A WALK ALONG THE APENNINES

Also by J. M. Scott

FROM SEA TO OCEAN: WALKING ALONG THE PYRENEES
(Geoffrey Bles)

OTHER BOOKS

Fiction
IN A BEAUTIFUL PEA-GREEN BOAT
HEATHER MARY
THE MAN WHO MADE WINE
SEA-WYF AND BISCUIT
THE DEVIL YOU DON'T

Non-fiction
GINO WATKINS: A BIOGRAPHY
THE TEA STORY
THE BOOK OF PALL MALL
THE WHITE POPPY

Children
WHITE MAGIC

A WALK ALONG THE APENNINES

by

J. M. SCOTT

GEOFFREY BLES
LONDON

A WALK ALONG THE APENNINES
is published by
GEOFFREY BLES, 59 Brompton Road, London SW3 1DS

ISBN: 0 7138 0540 4

© J. M. Scott, 1973

Printed in Great Britain by The Anchor Press Ltd.,
and bound by Wm. Brendon & Son Ltd,
both of Tiptree, Essex

CONTENTS

ILLUSTRATIONS

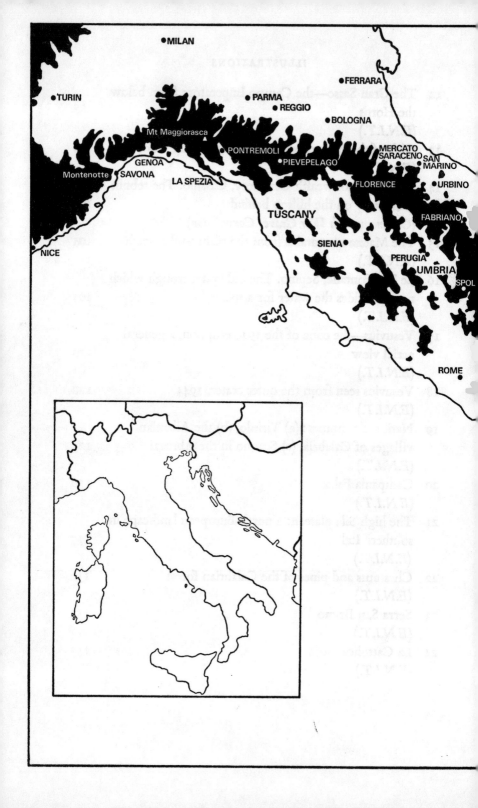

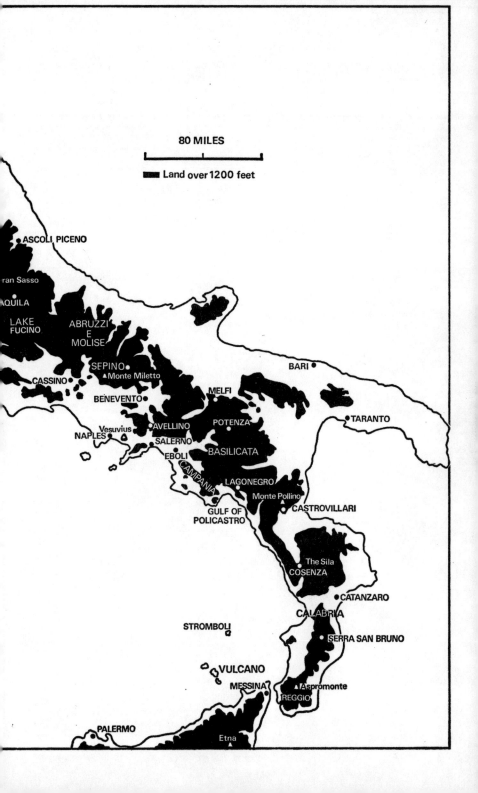

I

Montenotte to Genoa

All morning I climbed among sweet chestnuts, hazels, oaks and alders. I met no one. I was sweating but content, absorbed in the pure pleasure of the effort and thinking of nothing. Interest in the surroundings suddenly woke when the trees became stunted and scattered. And then with the suddenness of breaking surface after a deep dive I was blinking in the full August sunshine and had a splendid view. I turned about, and it was all around me.

I was standing on a summit which the map calls Tesoro—Treasure—but the local people Montenotte—Mountain of the Night. To the south was the purple Mediterranean stretching away and away until sky met water in a blur of haze. The Ligurian coast, the crowded Italian Riviera, was hidden; for the mountains rose suddenly from the sea and with their peaks, their forested slopes and herring-bone ridges they filled the other three quadrants of vision. But the ranges were differently named. To the west, beyond the few miles I had walked from the Pass of Cadibona, the Maritime Alps rose up to stretch along the entire Riviera and deeply into France. To the north, beyond more forested ridges which obscured the background, lay the Po Valley plain of Piedmont which runs up to the foot of the High Alps—Mont Blanc, the Matterhorn, Monte Rosa. Eastward of Montenotte there continued—or would begin—the great Chain of the Apennines which extends throughout the whole peninsula of Italy.

Since the days of Strabo, which roughly corresponded with the life of Christ on Earth, the traditional starting point of the Apennines has been the Pass of Cadibona. I say traditional because modern geographers and geologists, considering rocks, soil, altitude and topographical character of the mountains, have placed the start further to the east, at the Passo dei Giovi above Genoa. They dismiss the range between the Passes of Cadibona and Giovi as 'transitional', saying it was still under the sea when the Maritime Alps and the Apennines had already risen. But my map backed tradition by calling it the Ligurian Apennines. Since I meant to walk the whole length of the Appenines thirty or forty miles did not make much difference, so to be on the safe side I had started from Altare on the Pass of Cadibona.

The general course of the Apennines, and therefore of this book, is as follows. As the Tuscan Apennines they first run obliquely (south-eastwards) across the country, cutting off the valley of the Po and continental Italy from the leg-shaped peninsula.

Having drawn a line from the Gulf of Genoa almost to the Adriatic the Apennines turn southward down the leg, and since the leg is cocked at an angle to the lines of longitude the mountains trend towards the west coast again. Their crest forms the border between the Regions of Umbria and the Marches. They broaden out further south, almost filling the peninsula, and reach their greatest altitude in the Abruzzi. At the southern end of this part of the range, in the latitude of Rome, the high spur of the Matese juts eastward towards Gargano and the Adriatic while lesser mountains spread towards the west.

All the way southward from here the narrow land bulges with mountains as a Christmas stocking does with odd-shaped gifts. The only extensive plains fringe the Adriatic coast—around Bari, which is on the Achilles tendon, and on the Heel. For with the Campanian or Roman Apennines the range has attached itself to the west coast which it follows down the shin and instep, through

Lucania and Calabria, to the Toe. There this great and varied range ends in the lonely mass of Aspromonte.

I have used the familiar analogy of a leg and foot because it helps one to visualize the whole. But in this sense the difference of the Apennines from the bones of a leg is that they are longer than the leg. They only fit in by curving from side to side. Measured on a map they are about 750 miles long. For a man who would follow them on foot the distance to be covered is approximately double. It always is in mountains.

I was in for a long walk, one which could only be completed in a series of holidays. But I felt it was worthwhile. One must suppose that from the earliest times the Divine Planners had scheduled the Mediterranean as the cradle of civilization. It was a tidily shaped inland sea, its northern shore almost as symmetrically drawn as the African shore line. Then in the Tertiary Period Italy had to put her foot in it, or rather she raised it out of the water. It appeared from the sea not looking in the least like a leg of Venus but rather as a skeletal limb, a series of long rocky islands. These were to become the higher reaches of the Apennines. Still she raised her leg, disclosing lower reaches and connecting the whole with a flesh of foothills and plains. Thus the peninsula was born.

Speaking less fancifully, the Apennines are the oldest, most stable part of Italy. The people who live on the Apennines are likely to be derived from the oldest races, driven up there by invaders or local conquerers. In customs and ancient character they are certainly the richest, though poorest in worldly goods. I realized that of the legion of authors who have written about Italy, none has looked at the country from that point of view, from above downwards. As an uncultured person I was attracted by the idea that I would be above culture. Also I prefer country to towns, mountains to plains. From all this was born the resolve to walk by the high-level route from end to end.

Walk is a four-letter word which shocks most sophisticated people more than the other ones do. But you cannot see the Apennines without walking, for only over very short stretches does any road follow the chain: they prefer to cross it, and at the lowest points. Certainly there are many places where the walker must make a detour by road to avoid tiresome difficulties. But on the whole the Apennines are excellent walking country.

The eastern slopes of Montenotte were delightful, patchworked with clumps of trees and stretches of pasture bright with flowers. I came on a monument which said that Napoleon fought a battle there. It seemed a curious choice of place—pleasant for wandering but bad for fighting. The troops would be tired after the long climb, I thought, and would see little among the trees. But having no history in my pack I did not then know the story.

The Battle of Montenotte is interesting as being the first which Napoleon fought as a Commander-in-Chief. In March 1796 he married Josephine, and before the end of that same month he arrived in Nice to take command of the Army of Italy—for Nice, the birth-town of Garibaldi, was then in Italy.

The young C.-in-C. found 30,000 soldiers whose morale and physical condition were very low indeed. They were opposed by a combined army of Austrians and Piedmontese defending their own country. Napoleon issued a proclamation to his men. 'You are badly fed and all but naked . . . I am about to lead you into the most fertile plains in the world. Before you are great cities and rich provinces; there we shall find honour, glory, riches.' It was in this spirit that the sons of the Revolution which preached liberty, fraternity, equality, marched from the sea to cross the mountains which formed the border of Piedmont.

By a quick series of battles the Piedmontese were knocked out of the war, the Austrians were constricted in the fortress of Mantua, and Napoleon was in Milan demanding a heavy tribute of treasure and works of art. So whether or not Montenotte is the first mountain in the Apennine Chain it was a turning point of history. Napoleon said later that this swift campaign showed him for the first time that he was above the common run of humanity and capable of anything.

Near to the battlefield is the village of Montenotte Superiore, consisting of three or four houses. One of them called itself an *Osteria con Letti*—a hostelry with beds. I had not covered more than ten miles, but being soft I was tired; and when I saw the place in the distance I was tempted to stop there for the night, for the next village, Pontinvrea, was six or seven miles further on. But being cautious I called for wine and water before asking for a room. The drink, cold and sharp, was delicious after the heat of the day, but the place did not attract. So I went on, through pine trees and close beside a stream.

Pontinvrea had *pretese*, its pretensions being of a holiday resort, and it was the height of the holiday season. I was lucky to find a bed in a *locanda*, the lowest class of inn, but in this case clean and comfortable.

I did not expect that it would take long to reach Genoa from Pontinvrea, for the straight line distance is only about thirty miles. I thought that the young Apennines (or transitional mountains) would be mild and easy. In fact they are not high, rarely more than 3,000 feet. But they are exuberant and undisciplined. They have no intention of forming themselves into a neat little chain. They bounce up all over the place, following no predictable pattern. And rivers, large and small, have cut deep into the soft rock. That is why the ridges have that striking herringbone appearance. The roads must twist and turn like strings of spaghetti to get anywhere, and the walker cannot usefully take short cuts, for the woods are thick, precipices and gorges numerous.

To escape this exhausting maze I turned towards the coast and followed the balding hills above the sea, being forced right down whenever I came to a river. It was not particularly interesting country, and I will describe only one incident. I had walked all morning against a strong, warm wind, and found a sheltered place to lunch among fir trees and heath. There was a wonderful view of the sea, a smell of resin and flowers and the faint odour of a camp fire. I was happy and I became sleepy. Wind suddenly cut off has that effect; so does food and wine. I had to speak to myself seriously (I often think aloud when alone) to make me go on instead of going to sleep. I walked over the ridge which had sheltered me and faced an orange wall of fire with a crest of smoke. It was moving at remarkable speed, crackling through the thorn bushes, reaching out long tongues of flame to fir trees which caught fire with the noise of an explosion.

I got out of its way and ran down to the road. There I stopped three motorists and asked them to report the fire. Walking on down the road I came to the place where it had started, perhaps by a cigarette butt thrown from a car. Some time later the wail of a siren came up the road and a jeep full of *carabinieri* went racing by on their way to arrest the fire.

I regained the ridge and in due course reached the Passo dei Giovi. The Pass of Cadibona is crossed by a smallish road which runs inland from Savona, and it has a village called Altare, meaning altar, to give it a hint of romance. The Pass of the Joves is scarred by the autostrada running northward from Genoa. It is an unattractive place for a walker, but on the whole I prefer to accept it as the starting point of the Apennines. For in that case the Apennines have a root of rounded hills, their contours accentuated by lines of vines, which reach out northwards into the upper plain of the Po through Acqui, Alba and Asti. They include Monferrato which is made of vines (they grow wild in the hedges even) and they produce famous wines with sonorous names—Barbera,

Cortese, Grignolino, Dolcetto, Barolo. What better sap could feed a mountainous range? Asti Spumante even, it is not Champagne (it never claimed to be), but drink it in a chalet high above some Italian ski resort and you will make better patterns in the snow than you have ever done before.

From the Passo dei Giovi the steepness of the slopes and the number of converging valleys forced me down to Genoa. It must always have done the same to everybody thereabouts, and that is why Genoa has grown up into so great a port. It is a less good natural harbour than its neighbour La Spezia, for instance. All its shelter is artificial—a concrete basin, concrete wharves, even a concrete aerodrome built out into the sea. But the old town has its charm. The *caruggi*, narrow as lanes, wind between tall tenement buildings with washing waving gaily overhead.

In one of these I met a drunk. An inebriated Italian is so rare a bird that I stopped to look. He was shuffling along with glassy eyes fixed straight ahead, and he tried to walk through me as if I were an hallucination. I took him gently by the shoulders and turned him round, and he shuffled away as he had come.

The vast cemetery called Staglieno was on my route out of the town. It is laid out with considerable skill in a natural amphitheatre on a steep hillside. On the whole the finest graves—family vaults the size of chapels—are on the curving summit ridge. Most of them are in remarkably good taste. There are practically no angels such as spread their smog-blackened wings over the Cimitero Monumentale in Milan. The big tombs of the Staglieno are solid, worthy constructions. Occasionally, when there is a photograph on the memorial stone, one feels that the dead person must find it hard to die up to such a mass of masonry as covers him. That little fellow with a moustache—if he came out at night wouldn't he be worried? But on the whole the dead must be well satisfied with their accommodation.

The grave I liked best was of an athlete. His statue, rather more than life size, is in the attitude of running. His arms are outstretched as if he has just broken the tape, and there is a broad smile on his face. He is a pleasant contrast to the mourning figures.

From this high upper curve, this aristocratic suburb, one looks down on a crowded city. How little space each person takes and what a lot there are! Avenues run between the massed houses of the dead. And they are segregated. There is a large number—fifty or more—of *campi adulti*, fields of adults. There is a *campo infanti*, minute graves and mausoleums the size of dolls' houses. There is a *campo fanciulli*, of children, slightly bigger. God knows how many graves there are among the cypresses and holm oaks. I suppose it is these living trees which give kindliness to the scene, but it has great dignity of its own apart from the vegetation and the sweep of hillside.

Of course this population needs a considerable staff to look after it. Three workmen naked to the waist and burnt to bronze were laughing as they drank water from an ewer and spilled it over their hot bodies. One man was absorbedly polishing a marble tomb. Another was taking a few minutes off with a cigarette under a tree. There was nothing irreverent about this. Why, anyway, should one be more reverent to the dead than the living?—fear? I felt that these workmen helped the dead to keep a link with life. Otherwise they would be in danger of becoming idealised.

It was the orderliness of the whole that most impressed me. Living Italians are not strikingly orderly, but they spare neither time nor money to make sure their dead are. There are no anonymous mounds or even unweeded graves. An Italian may visit a cemetery every single day and spend more on a headstone and fresh flowers than on a year's rent. They take death seriously. I have not seen the Staglieno or the Monumentale on the Giorno dei Morti, 1st November. But I have seen numerous country graveyards where the same ceremony is observed on a smaller scale. Every grave is decked with flowers. On the Day of the Dead the devout may take flowers to a cemetery even if no loved one is there. At that season they are almost invariably chrysanthemums: that is why you should never give chrysanthemums to an Italian except in the association of death. At night every grave has a candle or lamp. The sky glows with them like Resurrection's dawn.

You learn a lot about national character by visiting the cemeteries.

As I walked on slowly under the sun my mind was full of a man more than two thousand years dead who showed a different form of filial devotion, spending his whole life in the fulfilment of a promise to his father—eternal hostility to Rome.

We all learned at school about Hannibal crossing the Alps with elephants, but the lesson generally stopped short of how he got past the next mountain barrier. By his sudden emergence from an unexpected alpine valley he achieved surprise and won two quick victories. But he was in the vast arena of the Po Valley, and two Roman armies were waiting to attack him as he crossed the Apennines where his formidable cavalry would be far less effective than they had been in the plain.

The Apennines overflow into the Ligurian Sea at Genoa: there is no coastal plain. But at the other end of the trans-peninsula stretch they do not quite reach the Aegean Sea. There is a comfortable gap between what are now San Marino and Rimini on the coast. The forerunner of the straightest road in Italy, the Via Emilia in the Po Valley, ran parallel with the range, just below the clean-cut northern foothills. It led directly to the Aegean gap and on the way offered several practicable passes over the Apennines which every modern Italian motorist knows. The Romans knew all this in the terms of 200 B.C. and of course they knew all about the arts of war. They had learned to respect Hannibal and therefore took it for granted that he would do the right thing—make for the Aegean gap or cross by one of the better passes, such as the Futa.

Hannibal knew all about the arts of war. He also knew about the Roman way of thought—which had been part of his education. With two fresh armies on tiptoe for his coming he could only hope to get south of the Apennines by outwitting the enemy. Therefore he did the wrong thing, the seemingly impossible. Riding the last elephant, he crossed the steep, untidy lumps of mountain which rise from the Ligurian Sea. Within a few miles of Genoa there are altitudes of over 3,000 feet, which gives some idea of the steepness of the slopes. Hannibal's men had about seventy miles of this, which is a long way to walk on the left side of your feet. Then for double that distance they waded through the marshes of the Arno before they reached dry land at Fiesole on the foothills above Florence. Thus Hannibal reached the central line of the peninsula.

I kept to the mountains, and in that way also achieved surprise in the places through which I passed.

This was *not* what I wanted. I wanted to be treated as normal by the people I met, so that they would talk to me as a normal individual as opposed to a *pazzo inglese*. 'When in Rome. . . .' When in Italy one must do as the Italians do, and I was doing as they don't. This was an unexpected difficulty which needs to be explained.

2

The Tuscan Apennines

Italy has an élite of mountaineers who have made quite as many
first ascents as the climbers of other countries, possibly more.
They spend nights slung in rope slings from pitons hammered
into cracks, and climb on next morning up sheer precipices. Also
a large number drive to the High Alps and Dolomites at the weekends, do daring and energetic things, and then drive back to the
towns again. But apart from these expressions of mountaineering
passione Italians do not walk for recreation—except, of course,
for the post-prandial or evening *passeggiata*. There will never be
any demand for an Apennine Way as there is for the British
Pennine Way. The names have the same Celtic derivation but the
two mountain chains are very differently considered. A wish to
walk the Italian Apennines appears as strange to an Italian as
would a desire to walk the Lunar Apennines.

I spent a night at Torriglia, about twenty-five miles north-
east of Genoa. This is a little holiday place for the not so rich, for
the moderately high mountain places (Torriglia is at about the
same altitude as Snowdon) are cheaper than the Riviera. But of
course everyone goes there by car or bus.

Next morning I was stuffing purchases of wine and food into
my pack when I noticed two properly dressed gentlemen watching me. One of them addressed me politely. The other throughout the conversation which followed remained silently observant.
'The Signore is not Italian?'

'No.'

'Where do you come from?'

'England.'

'You come by train?'

'No, I drove out to the Pass of Cadibona. I left the car near there.'

'You had trouble with the car?'

'No. I wanted to walk along the Apennines. I am on holiday.'

The two exchanged glances and there was a short silence.

'What is your car, Signore?'

'A Triumph.'

'How many kilometres does it do to the litre?'

I tried desperately to work it out, then had to admit that I did not know. This ended the conversation. It was painfully evident that they thought my car imaginary: if I had one, why walk? But how could I expect to be believed if I told the truth? I gave several miles of thought to the problem.

I walked uphill to Lago di Brugneto. This blue star-shaped piece of water looked very pretty on the map, set in the dark brown of mountains. It proved quite attractive in real life, but it would be much more so if it was not a reservoir—which means bare banks too steep for bathing. I would have liked to swim, for it was extremely hot. I said this to a man I met, who then told me that in winter they fish for trout through holes cut in the ice—as do the Eskimos. To such extremes does the temperature stretch even in the more modestly high Apennines, particularly in the north where the continental mass still has effect.

I went on sweatily up the valley—though temporarily downhill, having crossed a minor pass—to a little place called Loco. From there I bore to the right, uphill in earnest, to Fontanigorda. This is at the top of a lane which ends against the mountains—an ideal situation which will no doubt soon be altered by the restless ingenuity of road engineers. Meanwhile it is an extremely minor holiday hiding place offering no amenity except fresh air.

From the piazza where the baby Fiats were parked there was no view of the mountains through which I would have to find a way. So I went into the bar, ordered a bottle of ice-cold mineral water (the best drink when you are hot and thirsty), propped up my iron-shod stick, which skidded and clattered on to the tiled door, and spread my map on a table.

Immediately I was surrounded. 'È Inglese, lei? What are you doing?'

'I am concerned with a youth club,' I said. 'I have undertaken to conduct a party of bambini on an adventurous mountain walk. It seems that from here to Bedónia would be suitable—'

'That is impossible!'

'From the map it does not appear too steep.'

'Not for men. But for bambini— It is very long, and there is no road. Poveri bambini!'

I confessed that from lack of practice I had used the wrong word. These were very big bambini, and strong. Sympathy returned, and the Knowledgeable Man was sent for. I had hoped, as always, for local knowledge of interest—the sort of thing not to be found in guide books. I did not get any in this case. But I was given an excellent description of the route from Fontanigorda to Bedónia. It took me over a pass and through woods to the village of Rezzoaglio, and from there across the slopes of Monte Maggiorasca, which forms part of the Apennine crest, and finally down to Bedónia. It was the sort of good mountain walking that one finds in the Scottish Highlands. From Bedónia I went along a minor road ten miles or so to Borgo Taro, the Town on the River Taro.

This is a dilapidated little place, though not without interest. On my evening *passeggiata* I was struck by an old house in the Via

Nazionale. The façade was embossed with many crests and decorated with fascinating iron work. No one could tell me anything about it. The other thing which woke imagination was a memorial. It was of no particular artistic merit but was dedicated, 'To all the fallen and dispersed of all the wars'—a war memorial to end war memorials.

I woke next morning to thick mist. But this was not a serious disadvantage. The Apennine ridge hereabouts loops to the north, pushed up by a narrow valley which runs in from La Spezia. At Borgo I was not many miles from the ridge and might have followed it had there been any chance of a view. As it was I could cut across the head of the loop by following the line of the railway which points to a long tunnel, boring under the pass and coming out at Pontrémoli in the valley.

This is what I did, and there was no difficulty about it. The railway carries cars on open trucks, but there is a twisting little road over the pass, an unsophisticated track through the surface of which sprout grasses and flowers. It was lonely up there in the clouds. I saw no one on the road nor when, knowing the habits of such roads (and having a compass), I took a short cut through the trees. But it was not silent. There was a continuous *bang-bang* all around, for this was the first day of the hunting season. Next morning I read in the local newspaper that one man had been shot. It seemed a small bag for so many cartridges.

Beyond the pass the road surface improved. I dropped out of the cloud into rain, and was able to take more short cuts now that I could see further. There were glimpses of high mountains like well washed ghosts. Nearer at hand vines grew on long poles as opposed to the close-cropped things I had seen on the other side of the pass. I regained the railway as a train-load of cars appeared from the tunnel, clattering noisily. I found myself dinner and a bed in the close-packed town of Pontrémoli.

On my small-scale map I had drawn a ruler line from Genoa to San Marino where I meant to end the first stage of the walk. If the Apennines really ran straight from coast to coast their crest would have coincided with this line. But mountains never do anything precise. So far the crest and I had been north of the line. We both still were, though I was the nearer to it. But in the longitude of Pontrémoli the crest begins to trend southwards. By climbing onto the crest and following it I would come very close to the line at Monte la Nuda which stands above the Passo di Cerreto. This was a couple of days' walking to the east.

So I climbed out of the valley and across the southern slopes of Alpe di Succiso. I slept in a friendly little albergo at Casa di Giannino and next morning walked up to the Passo di Cerreto where a road goes over the crest between Alpe di Succiso and Monte la Nuda. Succiso may record a death of long ago, but there happen hereabouts to be a number of memorials to young partisans 'killed by the barbarous Germans' in 1944. (I have seen it authoritatively stated that 45,000 partisans were killed in Italy in 1943–45). One might think that German tourists would be put off by the memorials to many of these dead, but they outnumber all others.

At the café-restaurant on the pass I bought myself the unusual luxury of a proper lunch. Then in the hour of siesta I assaulted la Nuda. It is not actually a naked mountain for it wears a skirt of trees. It was all quite easy and the reward was great. From the 6,000-foot summit I had a tremendous view. To the north-west the bare ridge beyond the pass was soon eclipsed by Alpe di Succiso, which is higher than la Nuda. To the south-east (my direction) the ridge curved so that one could see more of it, entirely covered with a beech forest so thick that in the distance it looked like a green carpet draped over a wall. To the north lay Emilia-Romagna and the Po Valley; to the south Tuscany. But for haze I would certainly have seen the sea beyond Viareggio. Sitting alone there for an hour I changed my plan. I had meant to follow the ridge once it had conformed more or less with the straight line to San Marino, as it did here. But there were at least two good reasons for not following it. It would be difficult or impossible to find water; I did not carry much food, and if I were fool enough to break a leg no one would ever find me. Whatever I do in life I don't want to cause trouble when I am dead. The second reason was more practical. I would be as good as blindfold in that high forest. I would see neither Emilia-Romagna nor Tuscany. I would meet no one and practically no animals. That would be dull. Better to zigzag across the ridge, going down as far as the first farms and villages on either side. Thus I would see much and live on contrasts.

This I did during the following fortnight. I first went right down to Castelnuovo di Garfano which is at a mere 1,000-foot altitude in the Tuscan foothills. But the Tuscan miracle is worth a very long walk. The handsome old farms, the occasional melodramatic castles, the fine oxen, the olive groves, the way that every eminence is decorated with cypress trees—it is as if a goddess has been making a floral arrangement of the landscape. It is unique. Were I dropped by parachute at night, without even being told which continent I had been over, I would at once know whereabouts I was if I came down near a Tuscan vineyard. Throughout Italy they train the vines differently—from the neat, close-cropped French style of the north to the sweeping pergolas of Campania where a single cane may be longer than a cricket pitch. But only in Tuscany, or close to the borders of Tuscany, do they grow vines up maples. The practical advantages are that a living tree does not rot like a stake, and the maple's small root system does not interfere with the deep-sounding radicles of the vine. So one sees the vine winding sinuously round the rough-barked trunk of the maple, holding it closely for ever. It is a symbol of eternal love, not smug, for it is always gay, the tendrils twisting through the loved one's hair. Often it is positively naughty when a maple is embraced by two vines—*un ménage à trois*. A strong tree may even have three lovers. It is from this state of affairs that Chianti comes.

In Castelnuovo they were stripping the cobs of maize and drying the orange-coloured seeds on sheets spread on the pavements. They grind this *granoturco* into a flour called *farinata di polenta*. When boiled it is eaten, by the poor as a staple food, by the rich as a luxury. It must be flavoured with sentiment, for as nearly as any foodstuff can it has no taste at all. Italian millionaires become emotional when they see it on a menu at the grand hotel. There the head waiter puts a dollop on a plate already loaded with good things. Thus a simple national dish satisfies the primitive roots while tastier things divert the gastric juices: there is the illusion of living rough without the inconvenience of actually doing so.

Obviously I am biassed, and I have had many friendly quarrels with Italians on the subject. Actually, eaten as the exclusive food—as the Irish used to eat potatoes and the Scots oatmeal—polenta is just a belly filler, a fairly nourishing one. But gastronomically it is an excellent foil for rich yet subtle-tasting things like truffles and *funghi*. *Funghi* are not mushrooms; they are the many-coloured toadstools found among the dead leaves in woods, and at full season in September. *Polenta con funghi* is a famous dish.

As I climbed back through beech forest to the ridge, then worked my way through similar country for another ten days, I never had to invent a reason for my journey. Everyone who saw me was certain that he knew. My stick was for rootling and my pack for carrying the toadstools that I found.

When I was on a road a car would stop with a screech of brakes, eager faces were projected from the windows, and I was asked, 'Have you found *funghi*?' As I entered a village a bright-eyed man would come running from his house with, 'Salve, Capo, ha trovato funghi?' The trouble was that when I answered I had not, they thought I was being mean and keeping the whole great sackful to myself. Certainly I made no friends that way.

Wanting to make friends, and ever eager to make money, it occurred to me that I might as well gather the toadstools I kicked over. But that evening, in the window of a chemist's shop, I saw two posters illustrated in full colour. One was of the edible toadstools, the other of poisonous toadstools—or *funghi velenosi* in the more picturesque Italian. I stared for a long time at one poster and then the other, turning my head from left to right like someone watching a long rally at Wimbledon. I realized that I would never know which was which. So I gave up the idea. I did not want to leave a trail of death.

It was a twenty-mile walk back to the ridge, a longish way in mountains. But it was all lovely country, an infinity of trees—beech and chestnut and acacias—with here and there a wide slope of rich pasture. I was struck by how little life there was. In the whole day's walk I only saw half a dozen people, one herd of cows with clonking bells and one large flock of sheep. This last was on a grass track near the pass. There was an enormous empty lorry with a wooden ramp running down to the ground from the open back, the driver of the lorry, a shepherd with his dogs, and the flock of sheep which swayed with little movements here and there as if on the point of stampeding. The problem was evident—to get the sheep into the lorry. I paused to see how the solution would be attempted, for mountain shepherd dogs are guards, not herders.

It was done with perfect simplicity. The shepherd picked up a young lamb and walked up the ramp into the lorry. The mother sheep followed the shepherd and the whole flock followed the ewe.

Sentimental meat-eaters need not be concerned that this flock was doomed to slaughter. Every autumn there is a tremendous migration of both sheep and cattle from the high pastures to the low. It used always to be done on foot but it is now partly done by transport. One autumn I was ill for a month in a small albergo in the Italian Alps. I lay in bed with my clothes on, for it was cold. There were no visitors until one morning when cattle came swinging in with clonking bells suspended by broad straps from their necks. I watched from the window. The queen cow of each herd had a larger bell than the rest and walked with great assurance. Herd after herd they came, all day long, well over a thousand head of cattle on their way to the low pastures. And that evening the men who for four or five months had lived on milk and cheese began living instead on wine and song. It was not a quiet night, but it was a stimulating one.

Foco di Radici, a minor pass over the range, had two fair-sized hotels and nothing else. I don't think any guests were sleeping at either. The attraction of the place was winter sports, as I learned later from the picture postcards.

The reception man I spoke to looked with interest at my pack.

'The Signore carries a heavy load,' he remarked.

'Not more than I can help,' I said.

'Not more than he can dispose of?'

I did not understand, and followed him up to my room. When I had washed I went down to dinner. Although there were no other sleeping guests, several parties of motorists had stopped for a meal. There was a waiter in a white coat and all that.

Polenta con funghi was on the menu. I asked for it.

'Today there are no *funghi*,' the waiter said.

In no possible way could I be offended by his tone, but he managed to convey quite clearly that the fault was mine.

Next morning I went out and saw that the pass here was almost a summit of the ridge. Radici, Roots, is the name of the nearby mountain, they told me. But there are no high shoulders. I could not make out which was that contradiction in terms, Mount Roots.

I went on downhill, trending towards the northern side of the range. It was the same splendid and unexacting mountain country. Wandering slowly I looked at the flowers. There were bluebells, geraniums of the ragged robin sort, gentians, autumn crocuses. And there were plenty of thistles, some tall and handsome. I saw bundles of these by the wayside. I asked why they had been cut. 'For flowers,' I was told. These poor people were making a little money as best they could. I thought of the albergo where I had slept, where I had not particularly made friends but where I had learned that there were twelve in the family—husband, wife, sister-in-law, brother, grandfather, children of both sides of the family. They lived on a few weekends of skiing, plus passing traffic.

I walked downhill from early morning until afternoon in country much more populated by farmers and domestic animals than that through which I had climbed the day before. This was Emilia-Romagna. If I had gone considerably further downhill I would have reached the most fertile plain in Italy. The people who live there take food as seriously as do the French. The pig in a hundred metamorphoses reigns in the human stomach. Most of the dishes are rich as Croesus. But the unfortunate digestion is assisted by the local wines, Sangiovese and Lambrusco. Lambrusco is dark purple and it fizzes slightly when poured out. It is not a red Champagne. It is itself, Lambrusco. A beaker full of it really does have beaded bubbles winking at the brim. Its commonest fault is to be slightly sweet, but when dry and cold it is excellent.

I went down to these vineyards now and then, as I had to those of Tuscany. And when I was up among the views, too high for vines, the local wines came up to me. So I walked this stage of the range with Chianti on my right, Sangiovese and Lambrusco on my left—an admirable state of affairs.

Of course Chianti can be a far greater wine than Lambrusco. I say 'can be' because Chianti may be little better than a *vin ordinaire* or it may be a wine of quality. If it is the latter you are after, choose a bottle which bears either the sign of the cock (Consorzio per la Difesa del Vino Tipico del Chianti) or of the Putto, the naked baby with a load of grapes (Consorzio del Vino Chianti, Firenze). The most remarkable characteristic of Chianti is its length of life. I was once taken by Baron Ricasoli, proprietor of the famous Broglio vineyards, to see a friend who opened some bottle of wine more than a hundred years old. We tasted it at four o'clock in the afternoon. There may not have been anything particularly subtle about it, but it was certainly not going off. Unfortunately there were ladies in the party who chatted away as if we were drinking tea. I believe that when Eve gave the apple to Adam he chewed it thoughtfully and said, 'Good year, the 4004 B.C.' But she was babbling away about the leaf apron she was going to make.

My view during almost the whole day's walk from Foco di Radici was of a mountain called Libro Aperto. It is generally difficult to divine how a mountain got its name. The imagination of the namer was often as exaggerated as those of the classical shepherds who saw in the starry sky the Horse, the Swan, the Archer. But Libro Aperto could not be more appropriately named. It is a twin-peaked mountain. The slopes between the two peaks undulate symmetrically and meet in a central crease (a stream). It is an open book, set up on a great lectern against the sky. In winter skiers would write their shorthand on its snowy pages. When I saw them they were blank.

But I must go back to the food, just for a moment. Fruit came up to me. There were dessert grapes large as pigeons' eggs which went pop in the mouth with an explosion of deliciousness. Figs were just beginning to get ripe, green outside but blushing internally. There were pears, apples and peaches. In the humblest inn all these at that season are placed before you in a bowl and left for you to do your greediest to.

I was making that day for a little town called Pievepélago (*pieve* means church, but the word is now only employed—instead of chiesa—in place names). Pievepélago is quite a mouthful, and as I walked under the sun I childishly played with it, ringing the changes of its syllables. It was a dangerous thing to do.

I lay down under a tree for lunch. A countryman came by and paused to talk. Of course he asked where I was going. Without the slightest intention of being funny I said 'Pievepegalo—no, Pelepievolo—no, Pegipievolo—' And then could do nothing but laugh. He looked mildly surprised.

Pievepélago proved to be a resort out of season, with more hotels than guests. From there I climbed steeply to Abetone. On the way I passed through a village called Dogana, which of course means Customs. I guessed (it was fairly obvious) that before the reunification of Italy a century ago it had actually been a customs post. The villager who confirmed this added that it had also been a staging post where they changed horses. Poor beasts, they would need a rest on that long climb. I bet no one got out and walked!

A particular fascination of walking the Apennines is that one is always on or near a natural frontier, which was generally a national frontier not so long ago. Until 1870 Romagna was a part of the extensive Papal States, ruled by the Pope as by a temporal monarch. Tuscany was not even allied: it was hostile. So this part of the range was a frontier between two different countries.

The man with whom I was talking was well informed. 'He knows everything,' said one of the audience which had gathered round us. But he could not tell me why a village on the high slopes of Libro Aperto is called Ospitale. I was interested for I had passed an Ospitaletto near Monte la Nuda. In my diary that night I built up an ingenious theory that these villages were originally leper colonies, placed as far as possible from centres of population. When the last leper died this would be conveniently forgotten, for no one would be proud of it. But the theory did not quite work out, for the flourishing town to the west of San Remo is Ospedaletti. It certainly never was a leper colony. It just happened to have a hospital or two at a time when hospitals were rare enough for the word to be used as a place name. And yet, if that is the general explanation, the thing happened with remarkable frequency. Besides Ospedaletti on the Riviera there are six places called Ospedaletto, plus Ospedaletto Ugánio and Ospedaletto Lodigiano. There is Ospetale and Ospetale Monacale, and there are five places called Ospitaletto. Most of them are in the north; none is south of Rome. Most of them are in hills or mountains. If hospitals were so rare would they be sited where it was necessary to transport patients over rough tracks, often for long distances? Mountain air was long ago recognized as being good for tubercular patients but there were plenty of other forms of sickness. A writer may be blamed for posing a question for which he has found no answer, but unlike the Know-all of Dogana I don't pretend to know everything.

Abetone, at over 4,000 feet altitude and with high mountains on three sides of it, is the main ski resort of the Tuscan Apennines, within easy reach by car from Florence, Pistoia and Lucca. It is a picturesque village in spite of the number of hotels—empty in September. It is surrounded by a forest of beautiful fir trees (abete) from which Abetone takes its name—that is a simple one!

I woke to a world wrapped in wet cotton wool. But in mountains this is often the prelude to perfect weather. It was on that occasion. There followed two days of such delightful walking that my diary becomes quite poetic. At first I climbed among the tremendous fir trees, most of them straight and tall enough to make a mast for a thousand-ton windjammer. There were also beech woods where the trees grew so thickly that, seeking the light, they were almost as straight and tall. One has never heard 'smooth and sinuously swelling as a beech bole' used as a compliment to a woman. But it well might be. And the softness of leaf mould to walk on! If there is anything wrong with the Apennines it is the number of stones on the mule tracks. Here it was softer than the thickest pile carpet.

Above the trees I was on short grass, and by noon among the 6,000-footers of the range. The view was like that of an enormously stormy sea, wave after great wave of mountains stretching to the horizon. There was the same feeling of helpless lostness. But instead of the ugly roar of an ocean storm there was complete silence, utter peace. Fear gave way to awe, the extreme of appreciation. The mist of dawn had melted to leave crystal clarity and I felt that I could see the Alps. This of course was impossible, but that was my mood: there was no limit to vision.

Starting before the shops opened I had no food. This did not worry me in the least. If you take violent enough exercises, or if you are enthralled, you do not feel anything as vulgar as hunger. You only feel faint, eventually. I have very dear old friends in my village who, every time I go away with a pack, exhort me to have regular meals. I promise to do my best. But if your first object is to walk in mountains you cannot anchor yourself to restaurants and shops. Besides, it is morally bad for a stomach to give it all it wants as a matter of course. It becomes like a spoilt child or like one of those people to whom one has done small favours and who are soon offended if one falls short of the standard set. My stomach, when I take it for a walk—which is good for it—is grateful for a crust of bread after eight hours. When I give it a good dinner it sings songs of praise. As you value your digestion, teach your stomach to sit up and beg—and to say thank you for every mouthful.

Anyway, I was above food then. Gradually I came down to paths, to tracks, to little roads and villages. There was satisfaction in hitting them off. But I was regretful of what I left behind and would probably never see again. In that way, most strikingly, mountains differ from the ocean. They have individual characters, the ocean only moods.

I passed farm people with a wave of the hand or a brief greeting. The farm animals—except the dogs—ignored me. My most lively companions were lizards. I love lizards. When you see them full of life you may be sure that stone is hot to the touch, the earth warm. They are silent as the hills. They dart over the rocks quicker than quicksilver, straight up, horizontally, then vertically down. They pause to observe you with one eye while the other looks in the opposite direction; then off they go again and disappear as if they have evaporated. They are not creatures of the present. They take you back to the good old days when Italy was only the Apennines. Those tedious plains were still beneath the sea.

I came down eventually to Poretta Terme. The Terme means it is a spa. I have the keenest sympathy for anyone who goes to a mountain spa because he is diseased. But there were lots and lots of people in the rudest health. The town greeted me with a notice by the roadside, Evitare Rumori Inutili—Avoid Useless Noises. I went to bed wondering what noises are useful.

3

The High Way to San Marino

From Poretta I went to Castiglione dei Popoli. It was necessary at first to follow a road. A car driver stopped to offer me a lift, and I accepted. When in the Pyrenees I foreswore lifts, with good reason: had I accepted all I was offered I need hardly have walked a mile along a road. But in the northern two-thirds of Italy they do not often offer lifts, except to pretty girls.

I remember during the war an order coming down from on high that civilians were not to be carried in military vehicles. One day I was driving in a staff car behind a three-tonner. A very pretty girl was standing lonely and appealing by the roadside. The driver of the three-tonner stopped and reached out a hand to help her in. Immediately there appeared from behind the bushes father, mother, little sisters, little brothers, all carrying bundles. I did not take the driver's name. I felt that he had had his punishment.

The man who gave me a lift was small and fat and had protruding eyes. No doubt his motives for stopping were excellent, but curiosity was certainly among them. He at once asked me what I was doing, and I answered, 'Walking.'

'But there is a bus,' he protested.

'Not for me.'

'You have no money?'

'I have enough money.'

'Then why?'

I pointed meaningly at my stomach and told him that my doctor had ordered me to walk thirty kilometres a day.

At once he was all interest. 'Does it do good? Is it for the liver?' Then he let go of the wheel and flapped his fingers as a person may do when he has just washed and has no towel. It is the gesture of acceptance of impossibility. 'But thirty kilometres! Your doctor is a very hard man.'

The driver put me down within a mile of Lago di Suviana. This was in pretty surroundings, but the lake itself—a stretch of dammed water—was a little disappointing. From there I struck off the road. It was a misty day, and this time the damp clouds showed no inclination to disperse. I don't think I missed much, for this is a comparatively low and ordinary stretch of the range. The only difficulty came from having to struggle through thick copses of sweet chestnuts which had recently been cut and had sprouted again. In one of these my local map must have been brushed from under the flap of my pack. I was left with only a 1/500,000 map, a small scale to walk on, until I should get onto the next sheet. No map is much use on a misty day, however. My compass led me to Lago Brasimone—again dammed and disappointing. Then I was back on the road with a fine gorge on my left. Next to no one, I suppose, has heard of this gorge of the River Brasimone, or of a score of others in the Apennines. But they make the Cheddar Gorge look like small cheese.

From what I could see of it in the mist Castiglione was a picturesque little town. And I found a picturesque albergo set among trees in its own grounds. Peace, I thought. I went up to my room which was decorated with holy pictures. Peace and religion, I thought. In the lavatory there was a Bible, or rather a Vangelo. I was still more impressed.

Having washed I went down to write my diary in the lounge for half an hour before dinner. My fellow guests were a students' reading party, deeply engaged in study. But they all read aloud, and now and then one dashed across the room to argue a point with another. We went in to dinner. There was one waiter to twenty tables so the service was slow. The students started to throw *panini*, the little rolls which are so good to eat and even better as missiles. *Panem et circenses*, I thought, still trying to write my diary unconcernedly while the heirs of Ancient Rome held a gladiatorial contest with bread.

The walk from Paretta had been something of a day off, and there was nothing high or exacting directly ahead; but I now decided to step up my distances to reach the more interesting Alpe di San Benedetto.

Leaving Castiglione I passed the South African military cemetery. It is as different as can be imagined from the building plots and farmland around it. Laid out with rose beds and truly green lawns it looks down the now peaceful valley which leads to Bologna.

The mountains to the eastward were not high, but they were steep, untidily arranged and slashed by gorges. So I was constricted to the road as far as Baragazza where the Autostrada del Sole came into view. Strange and out of place it looked on its long white legs of reinforced concrete, with beetles scurrying along in both directions. I passed 300 feet beneath it, to climb gradually to its level and above by a little lane which wound through woodland towards the anciently used Futa Pass. This the autostrada disdains, preferring for its own engineering reasons to dive under the Apennines.

My lane was charming, but its leisurely winding tempted me to a short cut. This was a rash thing to attempt with a small-scale map, and I was soon in difficulties among deep-cut streams and thickets. At one stage, following a track which cannot have been used for years, I was bound Laocoön-like by a thousand brambles and stood thrashing with my stick until I could work forward inch by inch. Quite as obstructive, though less painful, was the wild clematis quaintly called traveller's joy. What joy is there in being tripped and tangled by wooden cords too strong to break? But on the whole it was a good short cut, not much longer than the road. It was interesting, for I saw many birds, including four pheasants which are rare in Italy. Birds as a whole are scarce. St Francis was at fault for making them tame. The almost ubiquitous notices saying that *la caccia* is reserved or forbidden do little to restrict shooting. Such country as I had struggled through is evidently more effective.

I came out near the Passo della Futa where the vegetation suddenly gave way to grey schistose rock. Here the Germans have a military cemetery. There is a memorial building of grotesque architecture, constructed of the grey rock. Everything is made of it, the gravestones from slabs, the paths from chippings —line upon line of grey stones, each with a name and number on it, no more, and never a flower or a blade of grass—soldiers lying at attention on parade in their uniform field grey.

I had thought of stopping on the pass, where there is a camping site; but not for anything would I have slept there, overpowered by this Gothic melancholy. The nearest alternative that my map suggested was ten miles further on. But I only paused to drink and eat something before starting for Firenzuola.

When you are fit, which I was beginning to be, you can walk almost indefinitely. It is not in the later stages pleasurable, but neither is it the opposite. You are out of the world where those definitions have meaning. You are taking a trip. You are vaguely conscious of your two legs swinging past each other while you float and jolt somewhere above them. On this stretch of minor road, mildly downhill, there was nothing to shake the flat soda-water of the conscious mind into a fizz. As well as I can

1. Altare where the Apennines unobtrusively begin.

2. Part of the children's graveyard at the Staglieno Cemetery.

3. Pine and beech at Abetone.

remember the country was windswept and eroded, almost without trees and with more bare earth than grass . . . I dozed off on my tiresomely restless feet.

Firenzuola woke me up. I passed under an archway through the walls and thought vaguely, a medieval town. It was four-square. The main streets were arcaded. And the narrow little streets were parallel or at right angles, and the whole square mass of buildings and humanity was not more than two hundred yards across—typically medieval. And then I thought, but these buildings are new. They were brand new. Some of them were still under construction—though with lashed poles for scaffolding and bricks carried in baskets up zigzagging ladders. Had I in my trance walked into the past of four or five hundred years ago?

I put up at an inn, fourth category, with plumbing which might well have been medieval. I spent an hour drinking cold wine and water and picking thorns out of my skin. Then I felt sufficiently refreshed to explore.

I wanted tobacco, but could not find a tobacconist. (Who was the Italian equivalent of Sir Walter Raleigh, and when did he live?) I explored further. On the new Town Hall there was a carved inscription, dated 1956, recording for posterity the death-less courage of the citizens of Firenzuola in the struggle for their ancient liberties. It referred by name to the mayor, Michele di Lando, and to Niccolò Machiavelli. It struck me as imaginative to build a town hall as a war memorial.

I went to the bar of my inn and asked about the war. The answers I received were vague, the speakers little interested.

'But you have a splendid war memorial,' I said. 'The Town Hall—'

They looked at me as at a fool. 'That is not to the last war. It is to the fighting of four hundred years ago.'

'And Machiavelli?'

'The great Machiavelli.'

I felt a fool. But I had explored the town fairly thoroughly and I was sure there was no other war memorial, or none to catch the eye.

'Were you not involved in the last war?' I asked.

'Oh, yes. Firenzuola was part of the Gothic Line. It was bombed by the Americans until there was not one stone upon another. Then it was sprayed by fighters with machine guns.'

'Were many killed?'

'One German soldier. All the civilians, and the Germans too, had received warning of the raid and had gone into the mountains. When it was over we came back.'

They returned and set about rebuilding their town exactly as it had been before. When they finished the new Town Hall they recorded not the recent little bit of trouble but—no doubt as had been done on the old Town Hall—the local wars of Macchiavelli's Florence. Nothing could more impress one with the agelessness of Italy, its eternal regionalism, and—the communists included—its conservatism where national pride is concerned.

The church clock struck twelve from which I knew, having been kept awake by it, that it was six o'clock. So I got up. At the Futa the ridge of the Apennines had turned northward to make a wide and wiggly pergola, and I was darned if I would follow it in all its idiosyncrasies. So I turned south. My right direction was south-east, towards the Alpe di San Benedetto, but I preferred to go round two sides of a triangle for three reasons. It was open, almost treeless farm land, and therefore the farmers would have seen me crossing their ploughed fields and would have objected. It was dull, the same wind-blown weathered slopes with more bare ground than grass. And it was clay which meant that each boot would soon be the centre of a football of soil.

I went south by the road over a minor pass which is named

Giogo di Scarperia. There is always some pleasure of contrast in crossing a pass, and here I got it to the full. From almost bare slopes I came down into the intense cultivation of fertile Tuscany. Vines grew with maples in the tableau of a dance. Ancient olives postured like beggars, like devout supplicants, like angry men, like broken-hearted women, like Japanese soldiers who stood with their insides cut right out, yet lived. There was every sort of vegetable—tomatoes, multi-coloured peppers, aubergines, fennels with their ferny leaves, beets, mere lettuces, and of course fruit trees. It was lovely and fascinating to the eye. But it was not easy to get across when I turned eastward from the road. Pick any Florentine Old Master with a background and try to work out a path across the landscape. It is difficult.

I took a room in a very modest country inn, and being tired was impatient at the lack of service. But I slept well and when I paid my bill the old girl gave me a glass of vino santo 'for the road', and I was ashamed of my impatience.

I climbed to the Passo di Muraglione, a windswept indentation of the ridge where a road goes over and there is a barrack-like hotel which however sold cold beer. And the view to the southeast was magnificent. It was this which interested me, for I was now close to the spine of the Alpe di San Benedetto, within a good day's walk of Monte Falterona.

Falterona is an unforgettable mountain. It is not very high, about 5,000 feet. But trees grow on it as closely as grass on a meadow, and a man on it takes his scale from them. He is an ant among flowers, and a mound is a mountain.

You fully appreciate the splendid views to be glimpsed from the ridges. Nothing much is to be seen from anywhere else. You can't see the wood for the trees. But from the occasional viewpoints you can see the world. It is like the childish game of keeping your eyes shut until the moment of surprise. And what a surprise—a great gulf, and then tiny dots which you recognize as houses, thin ribbons which are roads. I suppose part of the pleasure comes from getting things in proportion. It is better to be dwarfed and blinded by trees than by factories and houses.

The glimpses were rewarding both to north and south, for the Apennines hereabouts are wide. They fall in a great wooded sweep to Forlì on the Via Emilia. And from the southern edge of Falterona you get occasional long views over the valley of the infant Arno to the Tuscan range called Pratomagno, the big meadow, which lies east of Florence.

I had climbed Monte Falterona to find the source of the Arno. The right way to set about it, I suppose, would have been to start from an unmistakable point on the river and follow it up. But that would have taken me far out of my way—and downhill when I was already up. Also I might have chosen the wrong stream at any junction with a tributary for the two are sometimes scarcely distinguishable, particularly in forest where you can't see far. What I did was to wander through the upper levels and any streams I came on were much more likely to be baby tributaries than the baby Arno. So I failed. I did not think the search was worth another day. It was enough to have got to know the splendid mountain where the famous river is born.

But for those who would pin-point the source—which I am told is not signed in any way—there is this advice. Climb to Passo la Calla, the most south-easterly of the Benedetto passes. Here there is a monument to Dante, and within fifty yards of it a wooden café kept by an old couple who have lived on Monte Falterona all their lives. They are beyond acting as guides themselves, but given time they could produce one.

The Tiber rises only about twenty miles further along the Apennines. This is remarkable when you consider that the mouths of the two rivers are as far apart as Pisa is from Rome. From Passo la Calla you could by following the range reach the source of the Tiber in one exacting day of walking. But by road the distance must be sixty miles at least. In either case the first place to make for is Bagno di Romagna. To the south-east of Bagno is Balze, on Monte Fumaiolo. From there you can't go wrong. People will direct you, and there are signs.

In any case, by deviating a little southwards from the straight line—as I did—you come upon the river when already a considerable stream, in country where there are woods but no great blinding forest. It is thoroughly interesting to follow it up to its surprising source.

The biography of a river is best dealt with backwards, upstream. Everyone who has been to Rome knows the broad brown thing which meanders through it as if it owned the place. What most people may not know is the quality of its brownness. I remember towards the end of the war being given tea by a unit holding a position on the Tiber a good hundred miles north of Rome. Tea, you might think, being brown would conceal brownness: not a bit of it when made with Tiber water. Without pretending to be a connoisseur I believe I could recognize Tiber tea anywhere, preferably without tasting it.

The colour comes from mud, of course. But how does such a leisurely river pick up such a lot of mud? The Wye, for instance, flows quite briskly through the fertile vale of Herefordshire and yet remains clean enough for salmon. The Tiber lazes through Latium, lounges through Umbria; and you can hardly see the water for the mud.

The explanation is that it spends a fast youth in a soft countryside, and it would have to be twice as long to get rid of half the impurities it has picked up before it reaches the sea—where it long ago silted up the ancient harbour of Ostia. That is what you learn when you follow it to its source. And you learn something besides about the innocence of birth.

Before it has lived five miles the Tiber has cut itself a gorge rather than a valley. It is no torrent, but this is soft rock, easy soil. The mountainscape is herringbone patterned by the little river and its tributaries, the slopes wooded, the spines bare and white. Higher still it becomes Egyptian wadi country, even to the extent that many of the eroded lumps resemble the Sphinx. Finally the line turns northwards. The stream comes down a hillside clad with young beech trees planted to cover the nakedness of the land by the Corpo Forestale.

There is a signed path which is easy to follow and quite short. The spring is small: there is no great surge of water out of the earth. And the water is crystal clear. That, although perhaps quite easily explainable, is what strikes one most about the Tiber's source—an innocent little bubbling spring.

Above it is a pillar ten feet high, headed with an eagle, and with this inscription, 'Qui nasce il fiume sacro ai destini di Roma.'

I took a drink of it and poured my wine into the stream for the popoli romani.

Thirteen mules swung down the mountain track, laden with wood, daintily lifting their hooves and planting them firmly among the stones. The water whispered something in its own language.

The source of the Tiber is on the inside of the curve where the Apennines turn southward. San Marino is on the outside of that curve. I could without difficulty or much effort have reached San Marino in a day. But having tasted water I wanted one more river before ending this first stage of my walk. So I bore rather more northward and made for Mercato Saraceno on the way to the Rubicon.

Mercato has so little to offer that one wonders why the

Saracens came so far to give it their name. Now, it has not even an inn. I had been looking forward to arriving there for many miles and was too tired to go any further. Fortunately I knew from experience what to do on such occasions. Don't bother about a bed. Eat. Everything will be better after that.

So I enquired for a restaurant and was directed to a most unpromising-looking place. But, 'Si mangia bene, si paga poco,' I had been told. Anyway I had no choice.

One ate well, one paid little, and drank a bottle of red Sangiovese di Romagna which was more refreshing than any Chianti I had recently tasted. But a wine in need is a wine indeed. Afterwards, of course, the man who lived next door offered me a bed in his house. I don't know whom it was meant for. I had for companion an enormous doll dressed in pink, and there was lots of chiffon and cushions of brightly coloured artificial silk. But I slept like anything.

From Mercato (the market was in full swing when I left, offering every sort of fruit and vegetable) I climbed eastward onto a ridge and then walked north. I did so for half the day. This brought me to Sogliano al Rubicone, a pretty little hill town fast asleep after lunch. Many other hill towns drowsed in the open landscape. I also saw the River Rubicon a mile further on—a trickle fringed by briars and small trees. I followed it for five of its twenty-mile course to the sea, and it remained a trickle.

Nobody ever claimed, of course, that it is anything of a river. Some unnamed civil servant in Rome had made it part of the border between Italy and Cisalpine Gaul, and Julius Caesar led his legions over it without opposition. The Eighth Army had a much harder task to cross it (in the opposite direction) against Kesselring's troops nearly two thousand years later. Yet the unnamed civil servant should have his place in history alongside the Indian cartographer who, after working out someone else's vertical angles, rushed into General Everest's office exclaiming, 'Sir, I have discovered the highest mountain in the world!'

I climbed out of the shallow valley and in the afternoon haze saw a wedge-shaped monument of a mountain which could only be San Marino. It looked a long way off, but it was not to be resisted. I turned straight towards it across country.

There followed a *Pilgrim's Progress* march, up hill and down, across streams and through thickets. The remarkable peak was soon lost, of course, and thereafter for a long time only occasionally came into view. As I gradually approached, the light faded so that it seemed to remain as far away as ever. But I knew that if I stopped it would be very difficult to start again, so I kept going headlong.

Once I barged through a thicket of briars and cascaded down a steep bank into a farmyard full of turkeys. They raised their bubbling tumult, the dogs barked and the farmer ran out shouting. 'Evitare rumori inutili,' I said, and strode on.

When it became dark the mountain was a constellation of bright lights pointing up into the sky. It looked more than ever like the goal of Bunyan's pilgrim. But my burden had not fallen from me. It was heavier than ever, cutting into my shoulders.

A thought occurred to me. Suppose when we get to Heaven we don't like it. The prospectus we have of it does not particularly attract. Streets of gold must be very hard on the feet. And what will it be like to meet my father when I am older than he? When one is tired one plays with a silly idea in the most irresponsible way.

I could not see what flowers were at my feet, nor stones. I took to the road. It was fairly level going until the climb began. What a climb! The map says that Mount Titano on which the town stands is of only 2,700 feet altitude. It was a great deal higher that night.

I have noted before that when you concentrate everything on getting to a distant place you have no memory afterwards of the close approach to it. It remains a long way off until suddenly you have arrived. So it was on this occasion. I was sitting down to a meal and there was a bed waiting for me at only twenty feet greater altitude than the dining room.

4

The Marches

You have to be besotted with love of the human race, or entirely indifferent to it, to appreciate San Marino in the summer-time.

Monte Titano is as striking as any mountain of its size—a steeply inclined limestone outcrop which has broken off, leaving an almost sheer cliff on one side. In the rolling country between the Apennines and the sea it is a tremendous landmark, geologically imitated and scenically complemented by a number of lesser outcroppings. It offers wonderful views. On the high ridge above the precipice are three romantic fortresses. The town is well laid out and there are buildings of architectural merit. *But there are too many people*, too many visitors with cameras and underdeveloped faces. And they are catered for by too many souvenir shops stocked with knick-knacks of almost incredible vulgarity. There is even a fizzy wine which pretends to be native to the place. One imagines demons in dungeons pumping carbon dioxide into sugared water.

It is all our fault, of course, and of the man who invented buses. People have done much the same to Mont St Michel, Le Puy, and a number of other beautiful things and creatures. People want trophies to show their friends. So they shoot them with a camera or a gun. 'It's a lovely day, let's go out and kill something.'

But perhaps writing travel books is not entirely innocent. So enough of grumbling.

San Marino has an interesting history, which is however easy to look up, so it will be dealt with briefly. The hermit Marino was a fugitive from Diocletian. Only Heaven and the Vatican know how many saints that Emperor was responsible for: it is an example of a person achieving the opposite of what he intended. San Marino became a republic in A.D. 885 and has been independent ever since. It has an area of 23 square miles and a population of 16,000—not counting visitors.

From the high battlements I looked down towards the hazy sea. Turning westward I tried to retrace my walk of the day before. Turning south I reconnoitred the landscape for my further walk in that direction. But it all seemed small beer, for I thought of Garibaldi and the much greater walk he did.

In February 1849 the uncertain Pope, worried by the active longing for liberation which permeated the country, had retired to Gaeta in the Catholic kingdom of Naples. Rome, sick of the corrupt temporal rule of the Church, declared itself a republic, and Garibaldi with a force of partly trained volunteers marched in from the north to defend it. Mazzini followed as administrator, and for four months Rome was ruled justly.

The self-exiled Pope appealed to the Catholic countries for help. France, jealous of Austria which was all-powerful in the north of Italy, sent General Ouidinot with eight thousand men. Garibaldi's red-shirts drove them back. But a Great Power could not be seen to be defeated by a guerilla, and Ouidinot's forces were reinforced until by sheer weight they pushed through the gates of Rome.

So that battle was lost. But the Venetians were still resisting Austria. Garibaldi with four thousand volunteers slipped out of the other side of the city to go to their assistance.

The distance was approximately three hundred miles. Garibaldi with his underfed and battle-weary men attempted this on foot, with only a few units of cavalry to scout ahead. He slipped past the Spanish, Neapolitan and Austrian forces who had gone out to intercept him, and for temporary haven made for the independent Republic of San Marino.

I imagined the tired men seeing the tall landmark from afar as I had done. I pictured them reaching it, climbing it, and relaxing. They were safe. But Garibaldi was not content. With his beautiful Creole wife, Anita, and two hundred faithful men he pushed on to Cesenatico on the coast, a few miles north of the mouth of the Rubicon. There they commandeered fishing boats and sailed for Venice.

They were intercepted by an Austrian squadron and only a few of the party got ashore near Comacchio in the lagoons between Ravenna and the delta of the Po. With Austrian sailors following and Austrian soldiers, 'whitecoats', scouting the flat land, the leader gave orders that every man should fend for himself. In fact they were all caught and shot except for Garibaldi, Anita who by then was so ill that she had to be carried, and Captain Culiolo, commonly called Leggiero, who had been wounded in the leg and could only walk with difficulty.

Anita died in her husband's arms. Garibaldi and Leggiero set out to cross Italy. It is one of the most extraordinary escape stories on record. The two men had a rich prize upon their heads, dead or alive, and the country peoples had been warned that anyone who aided them would be shot. But the peasants, though sometimes afraid to help, would never betray. Leggiero in a cart or on a mule and Garibaldi walking, they passed near Firenzuola and crossed the Apennine ridge by or close to the Futa Pass. From there they eventually reached the coast of Tuscany opposite the Island of Elba, and got away by boat.

Except possibly for the invasion of Sicily with a thousand men, this is the most fantastic part of Garibaldi's wildly romantic story. He is the great national hero, the fighting architect of united

Italy. As such nearly every town in the country has named a street or piazza after him. But how many think of him as the greatest walker Italy ever had or is likely to have?

From San Marino I returned to England. I did the next stage of the walk in the following December, traversing the Region called in Italian le Marche (the *ch*, of course, is hard, and the final *e* pronounced as *ay*). This is a small region only about a hundred miles long. It borders with Tuscany and Romagna in the north, then runs its length between the sea and the crest of the Apennines which forms the border with Umbria, and in the south it lies against the Abruzzi.

The name of the Region derives from the Germanic *marka*—a frontier, border or limit. It is commonly said to be so called because at one time it formed the border of the Papal States. But I don't believe it ever did—except that when the Papal States stretched right across the peninsula from Rome their eastern limit was the sea coast of the Marches. The ancient name was Picenum. In the Iron Age the local people were Piceni. The Romans retained the name for the Region. Then came the Barbarian invasions, and the Holy Roman Emperors who were Germans, and the introduction into the language of Italy of the Germanic word *marka*. It is, of course, a word that we know well as mark or as the Scottish word march, a border between estates. It is also found in much the same form in Provençal and Spanish. By the tenth century the Region had divided in three parts—the areas governed by Ancona, Fermo and Camerino. It is not difficult to to accept that people spoke of the borders, the marches, of these three areas. So when the Region was reunited it became known as the Marches, le Marche. It could be as simple as that, but it is a pity there was no reversion to Picenum or Piceno which are more euphonic and appropriate.

The Marches, as we must call the Region (using the plural as a singular) offers what is probably the best Apennine area for winter walking. For the most part the mountains are not particularly high, and although the slopes fall from the crest quite steeply into Umbria they sprawl out towards the Adriatic Sea offering extensive picturesque foothills. And there are a lot of interesting towns. Under snow conditions I was likely to be forced down to the culture level, so was glad there should be places where I might relax and enjoy it.

I did not for my first night sleep in San Marino, choosing Veruccio, a few miles to the north, instead. It is an attractive little hill town, and I would not think ever overrun.

From there I walked to San Leo, through which (or below which) I would have passed had I in the summer gone straight from the source of the Tiber to San Marino. San Leo is a rock outcrop on a much smaller scale than Mount Titano but if anything more spectacular. The short, steep road up it was used by Dante as a comparison when describing the way up Mount Purgatory. It is crowned by a fine old fortress, has a charming church and a fairly modest inn—a delightful place altogether.

St Leo (the man) was a friend, I think the only friend, of St Marino—although of course neither of these was a saint in those days; that is essentially a posthumous honour. It is pleasant that the two friends should patronize similar rocks in sight of each other. But San Leo (the place) is remarkable in that it has not only a patron saint but also a patron sinner.

He was born Giuseppe Balsamo. He later took the much more impressive name of Conte Alessandro di Cagliostro. As a youth he was sent to a monastery where he became assistant to the apothecary. Thus he learned what there was to be known about chemistry—this was in the middle of the eighteenth century. He left the monastery, travelled in the Middle East, then married a beautiful woman of the same mind as himself. With her—a lovely wife is a wonderful cover—he visited and exploited the capitals of Europe as a spiritualist, alchemist, and necromancer. He had the elixir of eternal youth, which has always been a bestseller. He did very well in that age of credulity of all things 'scientific'. But for some reason he preached 'Egyptian free-masonry', in which there was no money and considerable danger. He was rash enough to do so in Rome. He was arrested and condemned to death. But instead of being executed he was imprisoned in the fortress of San Leo, and there after half a dozen years he died. His wife took the veil. He had started his life in a monastery and she ended hers in a convent.

I found my way by little roads to Urbino. There was snow and hard ice on the hills of Montefeltro, but in any case it was rarely either practicable or pleasant to leave the road. When there was not snow there was mud, and sometimes there were both. The mud of the Marches, although not of the colour quality of that of Umbria, is remarkably adhesive.

Urbino has ugly suburbs which make one appreciate all the more the pink and ochre beauty of the old town. How lovely mellowed bricks are, and how nasty new ones! It is a town of great dignity and self-assurance—also, of course, of history and architecture; but this may be left to the guide books. Urbino has a wide view over little hills to the smooth Apennine ridge.

My way was now towards this ridge, but involved a detour to Calmazzo because I wanted to see the Gola di Furlo. This, where the powerful River Candigliano has cut its way through 2,000 feet of limestone, is a spectacular gorge. The river was not thinking of the convenience of anybody else, and until the Romans came there was in the narrowest part of the gorge only rushing water between sheer cliffs. No one could pass.

Yet this was the line of the Via Flaminia which led from Rome to the Rubicon and thence to Cisalpine Gaul. So in the reign of

4. Firenzuola, a war-flattened town rebuilt to its original medieval plan.
5. Sparsely vegetated land and eroded hills east of Firenzuola.

6. The fortress of San Marino.

7. San Leo.

Vespasian, in A.D. 75, a gallery was cut, big enough for the legions to march through. The modern motor road has chopped it about a good deal. But the inscription remains. When people had to cut words in stone one can understand that they made them as short as possible. But in this case they went too far, and I am afraid it made me laugh: IMP CAESAR VESPASIANUS PONT MAX TRIB POT VII IMP XVII PP COS VII CENSOR FACIUND CURAVIT.

There was no more laughing that day. It came on to rain as Italy knows how when it makes up its mind to it, and the strong wind pouring through the gorge blew the rain straight in my face. After the place of the inscription, the gorge continues for some way, the mountains only gradually leaning back, and on that wild afternoon the cliffs had no tops for they disappeared into the cloud.

Hereabouts—surprisingly in such fierce scenery—the Via Flaminia is level. It does not begin seriously to climb before Cagli. Then it squiggles up to the crest to reach Scheggia in Umbria by a pass which can never have been anything like the obstacle of the needle's eye at Furlo.

It had been raining now for a couple of days. But on the top the weather changed; it turned to snow, which blunted perception on the next ten-mile stretch which is more or less parallel to the ridge. This ended at a cross-roads where Osteria del Gatto is marked even on a 1/500,000 map. In fact there is only a small restaurant and a little café. But the café is in a big old building which may well have been a stage post. The village of Fossato di Vico nearby offered accommodation. Then there was another short stretch, this time back over the ridge into the Marches and down to Fabriano.

The crest of Fabriano shows a blacksmith at his forge, but the town has been famous since the thirteenth century for hand-made paper of the highest quality. I remember Fabriano with gratitude because it was there that the sun came out and smiled from a blue sky.

What greater pleasure is there than brilliantly fine weather after bad? 'Sunny Italy'—the quotes belong to the travel agents who not infrequently go bankrupt—can have as horrid weather as any other country. Milan, for instance, is much foggier than London, and in August has a damp heat which is insupportable. Even the extreme south, as I shall tell, can be wilder than the west coast of Scotland at the same season. But now and then Italy switches on a perfect spring day in mid-winter, and for that one forgives it everything.

I remember that day's walk vividly although the country was almost certainly less fine, intrinsically, than that which I had been through in the last three nasty days.

I wrote in my diary that night that the countryside in winter was dressed in skin-tight vegetation which accentuated the sinuous slopes of the hills. The mountains were almost as smooth. They were never rugged, never overpowering. There were golden-leaved oak trees and dark green pines. The vines were trained as in Tuscany up maple trees. Some stalks were as thick as a strong man's arm or even his thigh. They clung with knotted muscles to the trees. The rocks were limestone with a vein of russet in it.

I remember eating lunch, sitting on a stone with my pack for insulation, feeling as far from lonely as it is possible to be when alone. That is stated negatively but it was positive. I was part of this bright, brisk countryside. I was in the best possible company. The poet who is in all of us appeared and pointed out the things which in an everyday mood I might have missed. This continued all day long. At evening the hills were painted golden by the setting sun and the valleys were full of purple shadows.

I reached Matelica which is the right place for anyone who

likes churches. There is a choice of them, and the one in the little piazza is intimate and gay. But I did not want to stop in Matelica. Having fuel of energy still remaining I went on to an albergo near Tolentino.

I had been told that Cingoli was singular and I wanted to see it, even though it meant doubling back some twenty miles. So next morning I followed farm tracks to a crossing of the River Potenza, and then continued in the same direction which would (or should) take me eventually on to the Cingoli road in the area which is pretentiously called Passo Grande.

It was as mad a short cut as I have ever taken. The madness was not in me, for a lane started me off in exactly the right direction. Then, after a couple of miles, it turned round and went back. (That is true!) So I struck across country. I slogged over fallow fields with ten pounds of clay on each boot. I reached another lane and optimistically shook off the mud. The lane ended at a farmhouse. The country was made up of little ploughed hills, with farmhouses here and there connected by wildly winding lanes. Such tracks as there were took one back almost to the starting point as surely as the paths in *Through the Looking Glass* Land. Any attempt to walk straight was frustrated by a stream too wide to jump, too deep to ford and with a thorny entanglement of bushes on both banks. To cut a long walk short, I reached the Cingoli road considerably to the south of the point intended. I was tired and cross, and half the short winter's day was gone.

Then it began to snow, with huge flakes coming down as fast as the leaves of a book when you flick through it. Climbing steadily the snow was soon deep, for there was already a foundation of the stuff, hard and slippery. One thought wistfully of a lift; but no car would have stopped, and been able to start again, on that endless hill. In any case there were no cars about.

Then I heard a motor engine behind me. I turned to see what

appeared to be a gunboat. It was a snow-plough of enormous size, and though I jumped the ditch I was showered by the wash.

A mile further on, where the road became for a short stretch almost level, I found the snow-plough at a halt. I was invited aboard, and climbed into the high cab with the driver and his mate. Suddenly—as comes about when walking—life was as delightful as it had been discouraging. The big vehicle barged along at what seemed a great pace. It collided with snowdrifts as a fast boat does with waves and sent them flying while the soft stuff rose like great white ostrich plumes to either side. The steering must have been extremely hard work, for the driver, a strong man, was fighting with the wheel all the time. But I just bounced about in the cab and laughed with childish pleasure while the white sea was thrown aside. And so in great style I drove into Cingoli. I had not been asked why I was walking there. Conversation had been impossible in the din.

Cingoli is one of the best of the hilltop towns. It certainly offers the best view: for good reason it is called Balcone delle Marche. Even in the uncertain weather next morning one could see far out over the plain which the Romans made a major granary and which is still rich farming land. The town is built entirely of stone which gives it homogeneity, and its Piazza Vittorio Emanuele II is memorable even in the land of piazze. I was told by an innkeeper that the Inglesi do not visit Cingoli in any number even in summer. I don't think the British are much inclined to visit the Marches at all, except for that long straight stretch of sandy beach, and then they have little idea of where they are except beside the sea. Whether they ought to explore the Region I am not quite sure. I enjoyed it even in bad weather, but it has less to offer than most parts of a country which has so much. The marchigiani have the reputation of being particularly hospitable and friendly. I did not find that so. Certainly they were not inhospitable or unfriendly; rather they were negative in their attitude to a stranger.

But the Marches do produce some interesting wine. There is Verdicchio dei Costelli di Jesi (Jesi is fifteen miles north of Cingoli). The name suggests that it is greenish but the colour is rather that of straw, perhaps slightly unripe straw with some chlorophyll still in it. There is also a Verdicchio di Matelica—the little town full of churches. The dry wine of both these types can be very good, both as an aperitif and with a light meal.

Of the red wines Rosso Piceno and, still more, Sangiovese well reward the taster.

I walked from Cingoli to Macerata, at first downhill, then on the flat. Comfortable farms stood back from the road; and on the north side, about halfway, there was a splendid fortified farm. From the southern side Tréia looked at me from its hilltop. There is a tendency—or rather there was in medieval times—to pile up as many buildings as possible on the steepest, smallest hill. They look picturesque and uncomfortable. Presumably they gave protection against bandits and malaria.

Macerata is on a hill. As I crossed the River Potenza in the valley below it the road all of a sudden was named Via del Teatro Romano, and there were circular ruins of Roman brick and stone mixed up with poor modern houses. In the old part of the village an ancient brick tower, reminiscent of the tower of the Palazzo Vecchio in Florence without the rest of the palace, had been built onto by a brick works. Classical and medieval and new are sometimes jumbled up together in this land so rich in antiquities where so many poor people live.

The guide book says that this place, once called Helvia Ricina, was a Roman city and was destroyed in the sixth or seventh century by the Visigoths. The inhabitants, having learned not to live in a valley, then founded Macerata.

I remember Macerata with mixed feelings. It must have been a delightful place before the age of the motor car. There is a maze of narrow medieval streets, cobbled and without pavements. But you cannot appreciate a medieval building when you are flattening yourself against it for your life. The only possible time to explore was during the lunch hour and subsequent siesta—not during the evening *passeggiata* when the population arm in arm ousted both the cars and me.

From Macerata I went southward through country which at first was rich and unmountainous as Herefordshire. But I was converging on the Apennine crest and the hill towns became more and more lofty.

The first of note was San Ginesio, a peaceful little place with a long history of wars. It comes high in the list of viewpoints and gives the first glimpse of the massive Monti Sibillini which form the south-western cornerstone of the Marches. Appropriately, if not very originally, San Ginésio calls itself Balcone dei Sibillini.

Some few miles on I reached Sarnano. Half the town is on the flat, modern and ordinary. Here I ate my second proper Italian lunch of the trip, and then—having nowhere to sleep—worked it off by climbing the old town which rises like a medieval lady's head-dress from the new. The steep, cobbled streets were narrow and often in tunnels, the houses joining overhead. It was eerily silent at that hour. On the top I was suddenly in a charming piazza among romanesque buildings of warm pink brick, a delightful church and clock-tower. But there was no view, for the hill is set in mountains: one is close against the range.

Again a ten-mile stretch, or rather less, and I was at Amándola, which is not a hilltop but a hillside town. The hills it is beside—not mountains yet—are still within the farming zone. But you can see the mountains stretching up beyond, of course. The little town is the usual mixture of new and very old, some of the old most handsome. And there is, I was told, a remarkable collection of manuscripts. There is nowhere to stay, not in the town itself. But a hotel modestly calling itself Paradiso is set on the hillside above and is as good as an ordinary human being can expect.

From Amándola there remained one stage only, to Ascoli Piceno near the southern border of the Marches. I made two stages of it by going via Montemonaco, a townlet on the slopes of the Monti Sibillini. I wanted to see an Italian named Michele Evangelista who was my driver twenty-five years ago. To meet again one's only chauffeur seemed adequate reason in itself for the 150 miles or so I had walked by my round-about route from San Marino.

I had a good stretch that day, though cold, over lumpy mountains the shape of cumulous clouds, which held up the real clouds. I reached Montemonaco in the evening, but Michael the Evangelist was not at home. So I put up in and with a mediocre albergo which should have been called Purgatorio.

The way on to Ascoli was unexciting but pleasant. The Sibillini Mountains look best from a distance. They are bald except for a few straggling grey hairs which are dry watercourses (except in times of thaw or rain) gouged out of the limestone. One which I ran down was full of fir trees, the fallen needles soft and slippery below one's feet, and smelling of Norway. It is nothing new to be transported a thousand miles in a moment by a scent, but it is always evocative. I came out on an unmetalled road which ran across the slope, holding its level in and out of valleys and gullies as faithfully as a contour line.

I spent only one night in Ascoli Piceno but it is one of my favourite Italian towns. It has the Renaissance fascination of Florence without the crowds. The buildings round its big piazza are all in sombre ochre shades. Hidden away unostentatiously in courtyards are some really beautiful palazzi. If it were not for the

Topolino and Vespa—the mouse-like cars and wasp-like motor bikes—it would be quiet. It has an air of dignity. When it comes to eating—which you arrive at as quickly as possible after a long walk—they like to give you *fritto misto ascolano*, a mixed grill with stuffed olives. Do not discourage them from this excellent inclination. To drink, Bianco Piceno and Rosso Piceno are just about equally good.

From Ascoli I took a train for Loreto. Not by the wildest stretch of imagination could one say that Loreto is in the Apennines: it is close to the coast, right down in the plain between Macerata and Ancona. But to accept its story requires the faith that can move mountains. Uncertain of that, I felt that I might at least move from the mountains to it.

This is the story. On 20th May 1291, shortly after the last crusade had failed, the farm workers of Rauniza, on the Dalmatian coast near Fiume, saw as they went home in the evening a small house on the Colle de Tersatto. No house had ever been there before. Within days thousands had been to look. It was a square brick building without foundations. It was simply furnished, with only a few terra-cotta vases for ornament. The roof was painted with pictures which told the life of Christ. There was a painted crucifix above an altar, and in a niche a wooden statue of the Madonna with the infant Christ in her arms.

Alessandro di Modruira, bishop of the diocese, was lying in his home, near death from sickness. The Virgin Mary appeared at his bedside and told him that the house was hers. It was that to which Gabriel had come to make the Annunciation, and in which Jesus had been brought up. The statue was an authentic likeness of herself, carved by St Luke in cedar wood from Lebanon. She had caused the house to be brought from Nazareth so that it might be safe from the Saracens. The bishop rose from his bed, completely cured, and explained the wonder.

Nicolò Frangipani, governor of Dalmatia, could not believe this. He sent four scholars to Nazareth. They located the foundations of Mary's house (nothing else remained) and measured them. The plan was exactly the same as that of the house on the Colle de Tersatto. The governor was then convinced like all the rest. Thousands upon thousands came from throughout the Balkans to see the Santa Casa.

On 10th December, 1294, after a stay of three years and seven months, the house vanished from Dalmatia. On the evening of the same day it was found by Italian shepherds in a lonely place near Recanati which is a day's walk north-east of Macerata. This isolated site became infested by robbers, and after only eight months the house again moved (according to tradition it was carried by angels) to a hilltop a few miles further north. Here it was on the land of two brothers who saw its business potential and quarrelled about ownership. A third time it moved or was moved, this time to its present site. Here it was on a highway and the town of Loreto grew up round it, a great church over it. It has remained there now for nearly seven centuries, and during every one of those years tens of thousands of pilgrims have visited it. It is the Lourdes of Italy, where the sick are brought to be healed. A marble covering now conceals the Santa Casa. This was erected for its safe keeping. It was on a Sunday that I visited the Sanctuary and I have never been in so dense a crowd.

There is also at Loreto a Polish military cemetery. This is small, full of flowers and dominated by a statue of the Virgin stylized in the convention of the Orthodox Church. She is tall, slim and calm. She does not look the sort of person who would worry about what Saracens or other sinners might do to her house on earth. And if she did decide to move it she would get it right first time.

When I picked up my car I made a quick tour of the Marches before going home. What struck me most was the geographical uniformity of this oblong region between the mountain crest and the sea. It is striped by rivers set almost equidistantly and parallel, their valleys separated by low hills. Of course there were hill towns here and there like irresponsibly placed exclamation marks. But everything below 2,000 feet was so carefully cultivated, so obviously belonging to someone, that the general effect was of convention.

I experienced nothing, of course, of the madly meandering tributaries, the muddy and surprisingly steep little hills, the thorny entanglements which are probably left there intentionally as barriers, marches between farms. You get to know two quite different districts when you explore the same one both by foot and by car.

What most excited me, however, were the views I obtained to the southward. The mountains fill Abruzzi to the brim. It looked like the best walking country so far. But for that I had to wait until the snow should melt.

5

The Abruzzi

From Ascoli Piceno in the summer I had a choice of routes to the Gran Sasso, the Great Stone, which pushes up the highest peak in the Apennines. The shorter way was straight south over Monte dei Fiori and Monte dei Campi, leading up to the Monti della Laga, which is directly opposite the Gran Sasso. But there is a deep valley between, in which is the town of Teramo; and a reconnaissance showed that the Mountain of Flowers and its neighbour did not live up to their names. They were naked except for their tattered fir coats, and the dry river beds were white as bones. So I went the longer way, starting south-westward. This took me back onto the true Apennine range which I had left in the winter at Monti Sibillini.

The southernmost peak of the Sibyl's range is Monte Vettore, a fine great thing like the Rock of Gibraltar carried shoulder high by other mountains. From its ridge it is downhill to Arquata on the River Tronto which is the border between the Marches and a tongue of Rome's Region, Lazio, which sticks out into the Abruzzi. From there my route continued to the south across the slopes of a mountain called Macera di Morte to the town of Amatrice.

Here are two names worth comment. The mountain is not of the smiling sort; it is for the most part bare and eroded, but the verb *macerare* means to macerate, or in a figurative sense to torment. It did not look as if it would do either of those things to the extent of killing one. Amatrice literally signifies a lady skilled in love. I saw no sign of her. There is, however, another possible interpretation. The masculine form of the word, amatore, not only means a great lover (such as Casanova) but also an amateur of the arts—one who buys artistic objects for his pleasure as opposed to a dilettante who must be something of a creative artist. If the feminine form of the word has a similar meaning I saw no sign of this lady either, and so can only say with the conventionality of a guide book that Amatrice is a picturesque little medieval town.

Talking of names, the Region which I was about to enter is called either Abruzzo and Molise or Abruzzi and Molese: I believe that the latter, the plural form, is used by those who think of the Abruzzo half of the Region as being itself divisible into two—an alpine Abruzzo and a flat maritime Abruzzo. But I have never found an official ruling as to which is correct, and only say Abruzzi because I prefer the sound.

A small road has fascination, particularly if it is faced by a steep climb and one wants to see how it manages this. A small unmetalled thing squirmed up the hillside south-eastward from Amatrice, and I followed it into the Abruzzi. Having got over the pass it dipped down to Lago di Campotosto, an extensive strip of water which makes a good foreground to the view of the Gran Sasso. But I was by then disappointed by my road. I had been very wrong in expecting it would be too small for traffic. A stream of little cars full of big Romans barked me out of the way, each raising a squirrel's trail of dust. I could tell they were Romans by the way they hooted, and was proved right by the Roma number plates. All Romans appear to be impatient, pleased with themselves and sure of themselves. I have never discovered why.

Beyond the lake I reached the River Vomono and followed its fine gorge towards the Adriatic until I reached Montório, where

I turned south. Having thus placed the Gran Sasso exactly in my path I had no alternative to climbing over it.

I put up in the village of Isola di Gran Sasso, which is near the roadhead. It is an interesting place. Most of the houses are tightly packed in the V formed by the junction of two rivers. This, I was told, is why it calls itself Island. But it is not an island, and still less is Isola San Biagio which I had passed near Montemonaco. I do not personally know any others, but Isola tacked onto some qualifying word is a fairly common place name, and I prefer a poetic and entirely unsubstantiated derivation: as an Englishman's home is his castle, so an Italian's village is his island.

The Touring Club Italiano guide told me that over many windows of old buildings in Isola there were incisive sentences in Latin, some optimistic, some pessimistic or wisely moral. I went to look for them along the narrow streets. At first I found only *Divieto di Affissione, Viva il Duce* (in several places) and two inscriptions over upper windows which were illegible from ground level. But finally I came upon BEATIQUIHABITAN-TINDOMOTVADNE—which translate who can.

The most pleasing experience was of another sort. Old men and women sat in many of the doorways, enjoying the evening cool. As I approached they looked at me suspiciously, even hostilely. But when I said 'Buona sera' their faces broke into smiles and they responded warmly.

When I got back to my albergo a wedding party which had been in full swing on my arrival was beginning to break up. The men, wearing thick dark suits so new, or little worn, that they looked as stiff as boards, filed past the bride to say good-bye; and to each of them she gave an artificial carnation with a bag of the sweets which Italians call confetti tied to the stalk. I have never seen a more self-conscious herd of men as they wandered off, twirling their flowers between work-hardened fingers.

Early next morning I walked up the last stretch of road, into a mountainscape most impressively laid out. Although the valley-head was horseshoe-shaped, the ridge proper, the watershed, was tangential, forming the whole horizon to the south and (as shown by the map) limiting a virtually uninhabited plateau some twenty miles by ten in extent. The slopes which led with increasing steepness to the ridge were carpeted with pine and beech forest to within a few hundred feet of the top. Set right in the middle of the view were the ochre-coloured monoliths of the Corno Grande and Corno Piccolo, the great and little horn. They rose in sheer precipices to nearly 10,000 feet, their limestone so bare and boldly carved that they reminded one of the Dolomites. All this was plainly before me during a three-mile walk. Then I was among the trees and could see nothing else.

The wanderings of that day scarcely deserve description. They were pleasant enough, for the sun was shining brightly, stippling the ground in the more open places. From below, the Vado di Corno (in Abruzzese *vado* means pass) had been pointed out to me as a nick in the steep ridge. But in over-confident carelessness I had not taken a compass bearing of it. I had been told there was a path, but I could not find it—only one which seemed to follow a contour right round the valley-head, going neither up nor down. I wasted a great deal of time in following it and in exploring rides cut by lumber men which looked like paths but led nowhere.

At last, coming on a stream below the bare face of the Corno Grande, I stopped. I put wine flask, tomatoes, grapes to cool in the water which must have come straight from a snowfield, and perhaps from the Ghiacciaio del Calderone, the only glacier in the Apennines. Cheese, salami and so on were placed in the shade of a rock. Then, sitting half naked in the sun which at that altitude was no more than pleasantly warm, I ate the best lunch anyone ever had.

Ruminating, I reviewed the problem. It was a waste of time to look for the elusive path. Better to scramble straight uphill and try to find a way over the ridge wherever I emerged from the trees. But first I must digest the meal . . .

When I woke the sun was low above the mountain rim. It was out of the question to go on, for if I could not find the way in daylight it was unlikely that I would succeed in the dark. Besides, it was not only a question of getting over the divide. Beyond it lay the Campo Imperatore on which the map showed no buildings apart from a chapel. I had been up there during the war, and retained a dim mental picture of a great expanse of natural inhospitality.

So I went down. Following the stream I came to a cottage where an old body was tending her cattle in a byre which was part of the building. She took me to the tomato patch and picked the best for the stranger. Then we sat and talked for a while among chickens and tame rabbits which lolloped about un-confined.

'Where do you come from?' she asked.

'England.'

'Where is that?'

She confessed she was illiterate. This evidently weighed on her for she mentioned it half a dozen times. Her brothers and sisters had been sent to school but she as the eldest had been kept at home. She had seen to it that her own children were educated. 'But don't have children,' she said earnestly. 'They bring nothing but trouble.'

Her smile was sad, and I asked no more.

It was still half dark when I woke at six next morning, so I knew the sky must be overcast. But if the weather was worse than the day before my sense of direction was better, and I hit off the track straight away. It was marked by blobs of red and yellow paint on trees and stones, one leading to another when once on the right line. The clouds were mobilizing overhead, and now and then I had to take shelter while raindrops pattered like drum-beats on the beech leaves. These were only preliminary skirmishes. The storm proper held its fire although, above the tree line, the wind gusts were sometimes so strong that I was nearly sent tumbling.

As I followed my track—now only a line of small cairns or perhaps a single stone placed on a boulder—I saw two muleteers converging on it from the right. We met just below the pass. The men were fine tough fellows. They had three mules laden with firewood and a foal running free. We talked briefly in a place of comparative shelter while they tightened the lashings of the loads. The nick of the *vado*, as narrow as a Pyrenean *porte*, had evidently been smoothed and widened. The men said that the engineers had done that because they wanted to find out what the rock was like underneath. It was something to do with the tunnel. (For reasons good or bad they are boring a road tunnel under the Gran Sasso.) I would have liked to ask much more, but the muleteers were evidently in a hurry. They told me, unasked, that there was a hotel an hour's distance on the other side. Then they went on.

Following, I saw the mules swing sideways as if dancing in the corridor of the pass. The men, one hand on an animal, put down their heads and shoved like rugger forwards in a scrum. And then the wind struck me. It was pouring through the gap with the force of a torrent, and much of its wetness too.

The storm broke at that moment with a barrage of thunder, lightning and hail. The ice stones were travelling horizontally. Once through the gateway of the pass they came at a more

8. The view from Cingoli in the Marches.

9. The church at Amatrice.

10. Monti Sibillini.

reasonable angle, and soon turned to rain as one descended. But the rain was out to rape. It swept up my poor little plastic mackintosh and in a moment had its cold fingers on my skin. Turning my back to it I saw the storm cloud sweeping over the ridge like smoke, as if the mountain was on fire. Flashes of lightning still licked the rocks.

A thunderstorm is much more effective when you are in it as opposed to under it. The claps are like gunfire and the lightning seems to play on you as a conductor. I was soon below it, but the wind was still strong and very wet. I set off running or walking with long strides for the hotel.

Two questions bothered me. Why had those two men been carrying logs over the pass? One is accustomed at the national road passes—the Mont Cenis and the Brenner, say—to see huge articulated lorries carrying wood in both directions. One supposes that is something to do with economics. But to struggle over a high mule pass with a load of logs ... That was soon explained. As the air cleared I saw that the great flat plateau of the Campo Imperatore was entirely without trees. If there were shepherds they would need fuel.

The second question was more subtle. Mules are sterile. They cannot have offspring. So what was that foal doing with those mules? I could not find an answer, but I became less interested as I grew more tired, cold, hungry and conscious of my wetness.

The hotel loomed up. It looked a whacking great place in the wilderness, and there was a flock of smart cars outside. There is only one thing to do on such occasions: create yourself a duke. I strutted in and asked for a room with a shower.

'Passaporto,' said the receptionist, unimpressed.

I fished out (the metaphor is appropriate) my British passport.

'Inglese,' said the receptionist with a flicker of understanding in his cool brown eyes.

A porter carried my pack upstairs. At the door of my room I asked him to wait and gave him my trousers with the request that they should be dried. I would have liked to give him the lot but did not want to presume too much, and I had in my pack spares of everything essential, which should be no more than damp. Then I telephoned for wine. It arrived as I finished my shower, and it tasted absolutely delicious.

I was content with it for three-quarters of an hour while I covered my upper half with moderately dry clothing and wrote my diary. Then, having eaten nothing since bread at breakfast, I began to feel really hungry. I picked up the house telephone again.

'Pronto,' said a voice.

'Io desidero i miei pantaloni.'

'Scusi?'

I repeated the request, explaining the circumstances.

'Subito,' said the voice.

Nothing happened suddenly, nothing happened at all. For the first few minutes I was amused by the situation. Here I was in a comfortable haven well above my usual standard, but held prisoner because I had no trousers. I remembered a poem by Samuel Butler, inspired by the discovery in the Montreal Museum that the Discobolus had been shut away in a dusty basement because the statue figure was naked and therefore improper. The theme was the custodian's explanation and the author's reaction to it.

> 'Discobolus is vulgar,
> Discobolus has no trousers.'
> Oh God! Oh Montreal!

I walked up and down, murmuring the lines. But my mind was

on my own trousers. They were of the thin, drip-dry sort which could have been made wearable in half an hour at most. My restless pacing took me nearer and nearer to the telephone, and at last I picked it up.

I was told that they were trying to identify the person to whom my trousers had been given. I replied that I had handed them to the porter, and that if he had passed them on for drying to someone else he would know who it was. They must find that person and bring my trousers. 'I want them within five minutes,' I said. Since I was cross, my Italian may have been difficult to understand, but I expressed my feelings clearly by the way I hung up.

In less than five minutes the telephone bell rang. My trousers had been given to a woman who was one of the cooks, and had since gone home because it was her night off. Her home was at Assergi, on the way to l'Aquila, and about twenty-five kilometres distant. She had gone in the hotel minibus. She had no telephone in her house but would be back first thing in the morning when I should have my trousers cleaned and pressed. No doubt she was working on them in her house at that very moment. She was a 'donna seria'.

We mock at the Italians for gesticulating. But in certain Italian circumstances we do just the same. I waved my free arm wildly while I demanded to know how the woman imagined I could manage without trousers. What about dinner, for instance?

The woman cook no doubt imagined that the English gentleman had another pair of trousers, said the infuriatingly calm voice. As for dinner, it could be served in my room without extra charge. The head waiter would come up at once to take my order.

After a moment of hesitation I declined the offer—for two reasons. Even in a restaurant, straight from the kitchen, Italian food is rarely more than warm and nearly always served on a cold plate. By the time the *pasta* reached my room it might be fit for sticking posters on the wall, but for nothing else. And I wanted a particularly good dinner. Secondly, and still more important, if I allowed the mystery of the trousers to be shelved it was likely to be forgotten. I did not entirely believe the neat story of the cook with a night off. I might be imprisoned indefinitely. So I shouted (to make the point clear) that my trousers must be recovered at once, from Assergi or the end of the world.

Having hung up I lay exhausted on the bed, thinking sad philosophical thoughts. The phrase, 'The person who wears the trousers,' means more than you suspect. The male who does not wear trousers is a nobody and helpless. You think of cars, trains, aeroplanes, medicine, the law, telegraphy, as essential. But compared with trousers they are all dispensable. If by black magic all trousers vanished overnight there would be no one—except women—to drive anything, no doctors in the hospitals, no judges, magistrates or policemen, no postmen and soon no telephones since the engineers are men. It would be much worse than a world-wide strike because all occupations and professions, all levels of society, would be affected. Discarding black magic there remained my own problem. 'She was a good cook as cooks go, and as cooks go she went.' She might have gone for good. I had no dressing gown and I was not going out in my see-through plastic mackintosh. How long would it take to have another pair of trousers bought and brought from distant l'Aquila? It was Saturday evening, Sunday tomorrow. Before I was properly clad some weekending journalist would hear the story in this talkative land. I could see the English headlines, 'Breechless Briton Stranded.' And a cynical article in one of the more literary Italian periodicals, 'L'Inglese Senza Pantaloni.'

The bell rang. They had got in touch with the woman through

a neighbour who had a telephone. She had not taken the trousers home but had put them in a cupboard, thinking there was no immediate hurry about dealing with them. They had now been found—as wet as ever.

'How long will it take to dry them?' I asked.

'Un'oretta'—a little hour, the voice said.

'It could be done in half that time.'

'We are much occupied with dinner.'

'I am much occupied with thoughts of it. You must do better than an hour.'

'The pantaloni could be ironed with a hot iron,' said the voice, thoughtfully. 'That would dry them a little.'

'I must have them within ten minutes,' I said, and rang off.

It is wonderful what hope can do. My thoughts became productive. I noted in my diary that the Women's Liberation Movement was wasting its time with all its meetings and discussions. What it should do was to plan carefully and execute expertly Operation De-bag. If it did so women could wrest the initiative from men absolutely and overnight.

There was a knock at the door, and an apologetic maid gave me my trousers. They were smooth as new, perfectly creased, and warm. But they were damp and they were still steaming when I went down to dinner, an arrogant male saved from starvation and shame by a habit-slave of a woman.

This hotel has witnessed another débâcle, if not de-bagging. Mussolini was confined here after his dismissal and the Italian armistice in the summer of 1943. But the Germans, thinking he might still be useful as a figurehead, sent in a glider party which rescued him without any trouble at all. On my former visit to the Gran Sasso I had seen the gliders on the Campo Imperatore.

The next morning was clear, the sun bright, and I walked the whole length of the Campo Imperatore from west to east. It is an unusual stretch of country to find at that altitude. It is all tundra and marshes, nothing much projecting. Even the Corno Grande and Corno Piccolo do not seem high since their rocky precipices start from well below the northern plateau edge. Monte Cristo and Mount Cinderella which are on the plateau look scarcely more than lumps although their summits reach 6,000 feet. You have the impression of being almost at sea level. The grass is rough as coastal salt-marsh grass, and at first glance is unadorned with flowers. There seems to be little animal life except for an occasional large flock of sheep which keep so close together as they graze that they make a single off-white blob on the off-green landscape. They are watched over by a shepherd who stands with his chin on his crook as a soldier does on his rifle butt at a lying-in-state, or squats tailor fashion with his dogs sharp-eared about him, watching your slow progress across his field of vision.

But the Campo is far from empty for those who do not only walk but also stand and stare. There is a variety of animals—no more bears or chamoix, unfortunately, but reputedly many wolves, hares, foxes, and marmots which whistle at you derisively like cockney youths. There are woodcock, partridges, hawks, and there are still eagles—the birds which gave their name to the capital of the Region, l'Aquila.

The Campo Imperatore, which appears level, in fact dips gradually to the east. After ten miles a considerable stream has formed itself out of the marshes; and after a dozen it goes tumbling over the edge. Climb to the Vado di Sole and the illusion of being at sea level is finally destroyed, for you are looking over a deep gorge at a tumble of lesser mountains rolling down to the Adriatic.

What may be considered as the tail of the Gran Sasso curls

round to the south and finally south-east, losing height all the way and ending just short of Popoli. At first it is semi-desert, spiny country which makes you think of a whole herd of prehistoric monsters. There is more rock than grass and the sharp little ridges are scaly with stones. A weathered boulder is a dragon's head. Here and there industrious peasants have cleared a patch to grow oats or barley, and there are a few sheep and goats watched over by a knitting woman or a dark-cloaked man who looks like the villain of a melodrama. The widely dispersed villages—Castel di Monte, Ofena, Capestrano with its yellow castle, are difficult to distinguish at any distance for they are built of the same rock that is all around. Passing through them they strike you as having remained unchanged for a thousand years. The longer you stay the more primitive they seem. There is nowhere that I would recommend a friend to pass the night.

I did not go as far as Popoli. I reached the main road which connects that town with Pescara. I boarded a bus for a few miles. One felt safer in a vehicle, for this is a great highway flowing with lorries and cars, a railway on one side and factories on both. The works of man are congested because the River Pescara, which road and railway have used to pioneer the way for them, divides the mountain system of the Gran Sasso from that of the Maiella, and there is not much room between.

At Tocco da Casaria, I took to my legs again and went south-ward up the little road which penetrates the V-shaped valley separating the minor range of Morrone from the Montagna di Maiella. This road took me to Caramanico Terme, where I meant to sleep. But the place smelt of rotten eggs because of its healing waters. These are so popular that there was no bed to be found. So I went on up the valley. This was a pity. Had I been able to stay at Caramanico I would next morning have climbed the Maielletta, the most northerly summit of the range, and had a magnificent ridge walk from there. I would also have passed a spot called Blockhaus. But the interest in this lies in the origin of the German name, and this I believe I have discovered. The ruins on the spot are of a building used by soldiers hunting bandits in the middle of last century. The Maiella was then within the Papal States, and these were swarming with Austrian soldiery, the Whitecoats who hunted Garibaldi. When the Italians were at last united under an Italian king they tried to rub out every trace of the foreign oppressors. But they overlooked Blockhaus. The only thing that puzzles me is what bandits were doing up there. I explored the southern half of the Maiella next day and had a good view to the north. A more unpromising place for banditry it would be impossible to imagine.

When you travel down the Italian peninsula by any means—particularly on foot because you then have time to notice details—there comes a moment when you realize that you have left the North and entered the South. I know that there is said to be Central Italy as well. But this is a myth. There are only North and South, both divisions varying in degrees of both temperament and climate. The realization that I was in the South came to me at the next village, Santa Eufemia, where I stopped for the night. As I entered the piazza the church bell was tolling. On either side of the church door was a wreath the size of a cartwheel. The *contadini* all in black were streaming into the church. I went into the albergo. There was nobody to be seen until I penetrated to the kitchen. There I was told that there was a room but that I could not have it until the *padrona* came down. It was six o'clock and she was still having her siesta. At last she appeared and showed me a room. I said I would have it when it had been cleaned and the sheets changed. She smiled sleepily at my fussiness.

Waiting, I walked up and down the dining room (there was no lounge). Outside it was a clear, fresh evening. The dining room was dim and fuggy, smelling of old food. The windows and Venetian shutters were closed. I opened them, then looked at my watch to see how long it would be before the inevitable happened. After 2 minutes 15 seconds the *padrona* came in. She was no longer languid: she was swift and decisive. She closed windows and shutters, then, pointing at a pram which was nearby, told me sternly that the cold air would harm the bambino. When she had gone the fancy took me to see this little troglodyte. I went and looked into the pram. It was empty.

I continued up the valley next morning, seeing no suitable approach to the Maiella before I reached the place where the Morrone and Maiella ranges meet at a pass called Guardo San Leonardo. There was a strange-looking albergo-ristorante here, and I decided to dump some of my load before climbing Monte Amaro, the highest Maiella mountain. The barman asked by which route I meant to climb. Would I attempt the *direttissima*? This is a term used for express trains and particularly difficult rock climbs. Neither seemed to apply to the modest slopes of Mount Bitter, but I listened condescendingly to his directions. It would have been wise to pay more attention.

The morning was perfect, the mountain high. I had that almost trembling feeling of excitement one always has at the beginning of anything which may be defined as adventurous. And Madre Maiella, as the locals call it, is a fine great lump of limestone, 7,000 feet high at Amaro, fifteen miles long and ten wide at its widest (it is lens-shaped). At first I climbed over open downland. Then there was a beech wood into which I plunged without bothering to look for a path. I have mentioned the delight of walking on rustling yellow leaves. But it was not at all like that here. The big trees had been felled some years before and young ones had come up thick and anyhow. Their branches interlocked from knee level to head level. I tried crawling, but the trees gripped my sack. One branch swept back and undid all my trouser buttons. 'You Italian beech!' I shouted.

It took an exhausting hour to get through the wood. Then I was on bare hillside, climbing a steepish slope covered with little stones. It was weary work, but I was cheered by the number of bright, delicate alpine plants among which the gentians looked almost vulgar. When I at last reached the ridge the little flowers were still with me, illuminating a moon landscape. Clouds swept close above my head on their ghostlike mission. It was lovely.

On the summit of Amaro is a huge red iron box—about 10 feet cube. This said it was the C.A.I. refuge. It was locked, a refuge only for members who presumably carry keys. But I had no wish to enter in any case. The view was magnificent, stretching for many mountainous miles to either side and in the other two directions up and down the range. It would, I repeat, be a splendid ridge to walk, with those flowers and that view. If it was clear you would see visions, and if it was cloudy you would dream dreams.

The descent was wild and stimulating. I ran down gullies where the stones slipped under my feet, carrying me with them. The noise they sometimes made was like a cataract. I have the doubtful reputation of going fast downhill, and I am sure that I have never gone downhill faster.

When I entered the albergo-ristorante to claim my belongings. I found two pairs of Italians refreshing themselves. They advanced on me with outstretched hands. 'Complimenti,' said the first. 'We watched you all the way through binoculars. How old are you?'

6

From Fucino to Cassino

In the latitude of the Maiella the Apennines are at their widest, reaching almost to Tivoli, the garden city of Rome—a straight-line distance of over seventy miles. I could not cover all that width of mountain or I would never get to the still distant Toe. But there is one curious bit of country almost in the middle line which I particularly wanted to see. So I turned west towards it.

From Guardo San Leonardo I went via Pacentro to Fonte d'Amore and Badia Morronese, thus avoiding Sulmona (I had nothing against Sulmona except that it was a town, and large). Fonte d'Amore is the site of Ovid's Fons Amoris near which a love potion used to be made. There is no sign of anything of that sort now. Badia Morronese contains a large square building. Pietro Angeleri da Isernia, also called Pietro Morrone lived here as a hermit towards the end of the thirteenth century. He became Pope Clement V, and in Badia built a monastery which was the home of the first Celestini monks. In the early nineteenth century the Ordine dei Celestini was suppressed, and the monastery became a penitentiary.

Dante gives Clement a bad time in the *Divine Comedy* (*Inferno*: Canto III, 60–61). He places him in the vestibule of Hell because the eighty-year-old Pope abdicated, which Dante considered a most cowardly act.

But the full story of Peter of Morrone shows that whatever he might have been he was no soft coward. As a hermit in the

Abruzzi, the Maiella and on Monte Morrone he lived in caves, practising an asceticism as strict as that of the early desert fathers. In such documents as he later signed he described himself as 'eremita'. He must have been physically strong, for one winter his followers had to drag him from his grotto when his clothes had become frozen to the rock. So strict was his rule against having anything to do with women that when the people of Sulmona wanted him to cure a six-year-old girl they found it necessary to dress her as a boy.

His election as Pope was strange indeed. The See had been vacant for two years when the College of Cardinals elected him in 1294. There had grown up a widespread belief that the Church could only be reformed by a pure and holy man—and who could be more free of sin than Peter of Morrone?

He was crowned in his own congregational church, Santa Maria di Collemaggio in l'Aquila, which he entered for the ceremony riding on an ass.

But he lacked the gift of leadership and felt himself inadequate as Pope. So he made way for the notorious Boniface VIII—in Dante's words 'fece per viltà il gran rifiuto'—made through cowardice the great renunciation.

As a simple priest again he was kept under surveillance and not allowed to return to his beloved mountains. He tried to escape to them, was captured and taken to Pope Boniface who kept him a prisoner until his death. He was canonized as St Celestine in 1313.

From a ridge ten miles east of Badia the stretch of country which had intrigued me since I first saw a large-scale map of Italy came into view. It even looks interesting on a road map, which is saying a lot. It is called Piana del Fucino or Conca del Fucino—the Plain or Hollow of the Fucino. It is represented on a map as a perfectly flat, low-level area, very roughly oval in shape which the scale shows to be about fifteen miles long by six or seven across at the widest part. It is patterned by straight criss-crossing roads and dykes except near the middle where there is a circle of road and dyke. Several streams are shown flowing into it but none out.

The real thing seen from a hilltop is just as surprising—this big, perfectly flat plain surrounded on all sides by much higher ground, most of it veritable mountain. If it can be compared to anything, Fucino is like a vast aerodrome which has been made unusable by dozens of ditches and tracks.

How it became what it is can best be explained (to those who do not know) by telling its story. It was a lake, a freak creation—freak because although water flowed in it could not be seen to flow out. It was a lake throughout almost the whole of its existence, a dangerous lake which might rise very suddenly, flooding an extensive area.

Julius Caesar is the first man on record to plan the draining of *Fucinus lacus*, the third largest lake in Italy. But Caesar became preoccupied by other problems. The Emperors Augustus, Tiberius and Caligula thought about it. Claudius undertook the task.

Thirty thousand slaves were set to work. In eleven years they dug a tunnel 5,653 metres long, connecting the western end of Lake Fucino (where Avezzano now is) with the River Liri which flowed south-eastward beyond a range of hills.

The work finished, Claudius felt that something out of the ordinary in the way of celebration was called for. He arranged for a battle on the lake between two fleets of galleys manned by 19,000 slaves. The two sides represented the navies of Sicily and Rhodes. They saluted the Emperor, then slaughtered or drowned each other. That finished, the flood gates were opened. But the result was an anti-climax, for only about a quarter of the water drained away.

So Claudius had the tunnel deepened, and celebrated the

second opening with a gladiatorial contest. Things went better on this occasion, but still fell short of complete success.

Trajan and Hadrian continued the work, greatly reducing the amount of water in the lake. Not only was the reclaimed land extremely fertile, but the rich began to build holiday villas on the neighbouring slopes, bringing money to a previously poor area. And there were no more floods.

So things continued until the Barbarian invasions interrupted the essential maintenance. Then the drain tunnel became choked and the lake began to refill. Thus the work which had cost tens of thousands of lives—for many labourer slaves had died in addition to those killed in the circuses—was brought to nothing and *Fucinus lacus* returned to its former state.

Italy's invaders and oppressors began the work all over again. Frederick II, Alfonso I of Aragon, Ferdinand IV all attempted re-drainage, but none was successful. So the eighteenth century came to an end with nothing achieved.

In the first half of the nineteenth century two or three private individuals launched companies to drain the lake, and went bankrupt as a result.

In 1854 Duke Alessandro Torlonia staked the whole of his enormous fortune on the project, declaring, 'Either I drain Fucino or Fucino drains me.' He started work on an enormous scale, with an army of workmen directed by the most skilful French engineers available. But they encountered hitherto unexpected difficulties. It became evident that Fucino was fed not only by the surface rivers but by springs and underground streams as well. The Duke was following the Roman plan of draining into the Liri, but it was found necessary to make the tunnel 20 metres in diameter and to supplement it with a canal and pumping station.

When the lake had been sufficiently emptied to start work upon its bottom a periphery canal was dug and a smaller circular canal surrounding the centre of the lake. In addition to these a rectilinear network of canals and ditches was excavated. Every one of these had a road or track beside it. In total there were (and are) 170 miles of road, 62 miles of main canals and 425 miles of secondary canals and ditches—in addition, of course, to approximately seven miles of tunnel.

The enormous enterprise was finished in 1887. It had taken the Duke's labour force of 4,000 workmen 24 years, and he himself had spent 43 million lire—when the lire was worth a great deal more than it is now. Torlonia was created Prince of Fucino by Victor Emmanuel II. His material reward was 41,300 acres of reclaimed land, of which he handed over 6,250 acres to the Commune for the use of the local people. Prince Funcino's reward was great, but considering his expenses in money and the fact that he had devoted more than half a working lifetime to the drainage his profit cannot have been excessive.

In 1951 de Gaspari's Government expropriated the Torlonia land in the Conca del Fucino as part of their agrarian reform programme.

Now, wandering in that dead flat plain, one feels that Fucino would make the ideal Purgatory for naughty mountaineers—walking round and round the periphery road with handsome mountains always in full view but never to be attained. There would be one consolation: although beet and corn are the main crops, the pebbly soil made fertile by so many corpses produces a lot of wine.

A day's walk south-eastward from Fucino takes one into the Parco Nazionale d'Abruzzi. But at the end of the day one may not realize that one has entered the Parco—and this is at first disappointing. The reason is that one has expected a park in the English sense or an area of outstanding natural beauty. The Parco Nazionale is neither. It is a stretch of country about 150 square miles in area, as wild as the Scottish Highlands though of quite different character. In 1862 it was reserved for the king to hunt in. In 1912 the Royal House renounced this right. In 1923 the reserve was declared a national park and hunting and fishing were forbidden. There are no fences or gates: the borders are natural—rivers and watersheds. Within these limits wild animals and plants are protected. Even the patient and generally unconsidered rocks are protected: the mountains may not be scarred by quarries. Otherwise ordinary life continues as in any thinly populated mountain district. There are farms, villages, shops, hotels. Cars bustle along the roads. If their drivers be unobservant they may not even know that they are in a reserve, for there are only occasional notices to say so.

But there are, by the most recent count, 1,141 species of plants, some of them found nowhere else in Italy. There is a greater variety of birds and wild animals even than in the Gran Sasso. Also there are a number of refuges which make long, rough walks practicable without the necessity of carrying a tent.

The borders of the National Park, being undefined except by description (as opposed to fences), do not matter. What is of interest is how best to explore the area. Two north-to-south roads run through its longer dimension. Although it is obvious that you cannot see the fauna and flora from a road these may be used, so to speak, as mobile bases from which to explore the mountains. Hereabouts I wandered without a definite plan. I will not precisely follow these wanderings, but admit that they were not thorough. I had not the time. One could spend several pleasurable holidays on foot in the park without putting a foot on the same spot twice. I was in passage, and this description is from that that point of view.

The entry if you come from Sulmona is by the road through Anversa d'Abruzzi, SS 479. You start in foothill farmland.

11.   The Gran Sasso—the Corno Grande and the Corno Piccolo.

12.   The Gran Sasso—the Campo Imperatore from below the Horns.

13. Girls of the Abruzzi spinning and winding wool.

Beyond Anversa you are in sterner surroundings; the road is cut out of rock above the gorge of the River Sagittario. This zodiacal stream is short, but it makes its mark on the world, cutting deep. It comes from the Lago di Scanno which is prettier than the usual run of hydro-electric slaves. It has a couple of nice-looking hotels beside it, but as happens too often when one finds an attractive inn it was the wrong time of day to stop.

A mile or so above the lake is the village of Scanno. It probably calls itself a town, for the Italian conception of a town (Città) is nearer to the Irish than the English or Scottish. It certainly now claims to be a winter sports resort. This is sinister. Too often in the Abruzzi and elsewhere one sees a place advertised on a roadside hoarding for *sport invernale*. I came to read it as *sport infernale*; for much as I enjoy skiing—or used to—there is nothing like it for destroying the character of a mountain village, turning it into a promenade of boutiques, the roads full of people in après ski outfits and staying in huge hotels. Scanno has not yet come to that. It is still a mountain village—or town.

It has the reputation of possessing the most beautiful women in Abruzzi. Undoubtedly many of them are handsome physical specimens. But beauty is in the eye of the beholder, and to mine they are too powerfully built. I would be afraid of meeting them on a dark night.

The local costume, however, long-skirted and tight-waisted, would make the sturdiest girl look tall. It is gaily coloured—blue and black and red—and worn with a wealth of gold ornaments which must be worth a fortune. The head-dress, apparently concocted out of scarves, has an Elizabethan look. One suspects from its flat top that it originally had the utilitarian purpose of supporting and padding a head load. The women still carry loads on their heads and walk with the grace that comes therefrom. The pity is that they now only wear the costume for the great church festivals and for weddings, so unless you time your visit carefully you are unlikely to see them dressed up. But you can always buy a picture postcard.

I do not know what Scanno is like for skiing, but it is an excellent walking centre. Two of the longest walks are to Pescasseroli (of which more later) and to Roccaraso which lies south-east, on a parallel road (SS 17). Raso means shaven, smooth, and also satin. The rock of Roccaraso is limestone as rough as any other, so I suppose the description refers to the mountains as a whole. They are smooth rather than rugged, which makes for easy walking.

When I left Scanno I went to Villetta Barrea, at the head of the Lago di Barrea. Although a road walk I enjoyed it for there were many opportunities for the game of taking short-cuts. The country was well wooded and always pleasant if not remarkably beautiful. I stayed at the little Albergo Pineta, and remember it chiefly because while I ate my supper an austere gentleman on the television screen told me that a big area of low pressure then centred over Great Britain would move to Italy bringing 'tempo brutto, molto disturbato'. One felt that it might have had the good taste to stay at home. It is worth adding that, if it moved as forecast, Italy cured it of its depression and the weather remained fine.

Villetta Barrea is on SS 83 which follows the upper course of the River Sangro first west and then north to the source, thus indicating—although actually penetrating—first the southern end of the park and then its western side. The border area south of the Sangro is the most spectacular part of the Parco Nazionale. A few miles west of Villetta Barrea an asphalt side road branches off to the south. It leads after a mile or so to a big black car park with coffee and ice-cream stalls and a souvenir shop. There was here a great crowd of holiday-makers. Boys were kicking a football about. Little girls were being shouted at. At the further end of the crowd a fat man sat on a stone padded by a cushion. His trousers were pulled up to show hairy legs, on his lap was a piled plate of spaghetti, a napkin was tucked into his collar and on his face was an expression of concentrated satisfaction. But beyond this man was a wonderful semi-circle of wooded slopes rising to castellated peaks where there was no one to disturb the chamois because, thank God, the human race is gregarious. These steep slopes lead up to the Camosciara where there are ample mountains, extensive beech woods and silent beauty.

I guess that it is hereabouts they take the publicity photographs of the National Park. Let them. The area is not typical of the National Park which is elsewhere unphotogenic. But this hint about Camosciara is given in confidence to those who would appreciate it, and with confidence for no one unwilling to climb could see it and no one willing to climb would spoil it. Nature puts her true devotees through severe initiation rites.

To complete this rough sketch of the National Park we will continue up SS 83 until the Conca del Fucino once more comes into view. The road turns north near Opi, an old town which stands aside upon a hill so that few pass through it and certainly no tourists stay. Three miles north of Opi is Pescasseroli. Half of this is old, unbeautiful town, the other half a highly polished resort with a number of expensive hotels. There are ski lifts on the slopes for fast downhill-only skiing. In summer there are lovely walks along bare ridges above beech forest.

The upper Sangro (north of Pescasseroli) is a small clear stream, going briskly but not rushing over rapids or jumping over falls. The hills on either side are at their lower levels covered with trees, chiefly oaks, stunted by the wind. There are stretches of pasture at the valley bottom, but very few houses. It is a lonely road. One reaches the source of the Sangro shortly before the pass. Then the road descends, twisting and turning, until Fucino appears—a bare description this, but the country is bare except for the wind-battered trees.

A mile or two eastward of the source of the Sangro is the summit of Monte Pietra Gentile. That is an appropriate name for one of the park's mountains. They are inclined to be stony but they are as polite as a stone can be. From the summit the intelligent walker heading south strikes cross-country for Villetta Barrea and so out of the park.

Before leaving it—the best guide for mountain walking I have found (I did not have it with me when I was there) is that of the Club Alpino Italiano, entitled *Appennino Centrale* (the Italians give the range two p's). It is not translated into English, but it is as well to gain at least a smattering of Italian before visiting Italy. You would lose a lot otherwise. Italian is the easiest language to speak badly, also the most rewarding. At long last that Latin you learned at school comes in useful! And the people—unlike the French who get cross when they hear their tongue twisted—are amused by and helpful, even complimentary to a stutterer.

This has been a wandering chapter, and so it will be to the end. I wanted to see Cassino again. The wish had nothing to do with my walk yet was not inappropriate to it, for Cassino is still in the Apennines, at the extreme edge of the Roman side. From a western outpost of the range the monastery on its hilltop 1,700 feet high looks out across the narrow plain to the Monti Aurunchi which are on the other side of the plain, close to the Tyrrhenian Sea. The narrow plain is now threaded by the Autostrada del Sole. It has always carried the road from the south to Rome. This high road passes through the evening shadow of Cassino's hill. That is why the monastery with its view of scores of miles was of such tactical importance during the Italian campaign.

To reach it from where I was it was necessary to cross the spine of the range and follow some forty miles of twisting mountain roads—a good walk no doubt, but I did it by transport.

There was the monastery of Cassino gleaming white on its hilltop, the substantial ghost of its former self. For the Americans rebuilt it exactly as it was before in homage to the sanctuary which their bombers destroyed. How thoroughly they destroyed it! Quite apart from Allied shells the monastery and town received 1,400 tons of bombs. When I had last been at Cassino the little town, which is at the bottom of the hill, had been a pile of rubble. And the monastery above was more ragged than the mountain.

By any law or rule of conduct the Americans were justified in destroying the old monastery. 'If thine eye offend thee, pluck it out.' Surely one may therefore blow out the enemy's eye. The Germans used the monastery as an observation post and fortress, with the result that their guns could kill unerringly. Although it may be of no more than academic interest the original monastery was built as a stronghold. St Benedict sited it there for defence against the Barbarians in the year 529. In 589 the Longobards destroyed it. In 884 the Saracens destroyed it. In 1349 it was destroyed by an earthquake. In 1866 it was dissolved, but remained valuable as a theological seminary with its library of 40,000 books, its architecture, frescoes, mosaics, and pictures.

I have no right or reason to re-tell the story of the fighting which went on in the rubble throughout the spring of 1944. It can be looked up easily enough. The town is now a new town, spacious and prospering and with a considerable tourist trade. The monastery is shining new. There are no scars. Only the cemeteries with their many thousands of graves remain to show the cost.

The Polish cemetery is seen to best effect from the entrance to the monastery—and it is tremendously moving. A wide avenue sweeps up a slope to a clump of trees which make a cross. Below this the graves, row upon row, are arranged in a great curve. One can only go to the graves on foot, and the long walk up to them with the details becoming plain one by one has a powerful effect on the imagination. It is very sad, very noble, very proud. The German cemetery suggests that the dead soldiers are still powerful, almost that they might rise in their ranks at the word of command and recapture Cassino. The British Commonwealth cemetery, as a townsman put it, is the most *signorile*, a word with a more subtle meaning than the dictionary translation, gentlemanly. This is a clean, green, peaceful place. Inevitably Rupert Brooke's *Soldier* comes to mind.

> If I should die, think only this of me:
> That there's some corner of a foreign field
> That is for ever England.

By temperament and sympathy it was natural, I suppose, that I should be most moved by this particular corner of Italy. But there was one Polish grave that I wished I could find. I could not. There were so many, and I did not remember Jan's surname. I doubt if I ever really knew it for it sounded to British ears more like a sneeze than a word. That's why we called him Jan.

How I got to know him demands preface. We had a mountain warfare school at Sepino in the Matese mountains further south. We used to train cadres there and also to send what we called Mountain Circuses to help units fighting in the Apennines, giving them hints on mountaincraft while they were on patrol. It was there that I got to know Lieutenant-Colonel John Hunt when he commanded a special force in the Maiella. Had I known that he was later to lead the successful Mount Everest Expedition I would have deserted to the enemy from sheer embarrassment. But that is by the way. At the beginning of 1944, with Cassino boiling up, we were particularly busy, for not only Mount Cassino but a good slice of wild Apennines was involved. Besides Commonwealth students we began to get Poles. Here language was the difficulty. I found that most of the Poles came from the German-speaking provinces, so put a German-speaking English officer in charge of them.

Going round to see how they were getting on I found them communicating in very bad Italian. I said nothing at the time but afterwards asked the reason. I was told that the Poles refused to speak or even to understand German.

The only answer seemed to lie in the attachment of an English-speaking Polish officer whom we could train and who thereafter could take charge of the Polish cadres. I asked for this.

We led a fairly unconventional life, often enough sleeping out. But when at the school we dined formally. One evening when we were already at table a man appeared in the doorway, stood for a moment in doubt, then came up to me, bowed and apologized for being late. I told him to find a place and have some food.

This was Jan. Everyone liked him enormously. He was so courteous, so anxious to do the right thing, and at the same time so boyish. Being shy he was slow to make friends, slow but thorough. Gradually he became intimate with the officers of his rank. He blossomed. This young man whose eyes never quite lost their sadness, or their resolve, was the life and soul of any group in the mess. It was moving.

Me, although then quite young, he seemed to consider as a father figure, and above all as a commanding officer. I could not get through to him as a person. It was via his British colleagues that I heard his story. I regret that I am now vague about it, for it was like that of so many of his compatriots. After fighting the Germans in his own country until the last, he had escaped, and after many adventures, had reached England to join the Free Polish Forces. He did not know if any of his family was still alive. He believed them dead. He had no home, no money of course except his pay, nothing but the resolve to help defeat Germany and so liberate his country. This was the soul of him, austere to the point of being sacrificial; but as I have said he was a boy and among those of his own age he was the best possible company. There were no end of Jan stories.

He was the devil to train. He was keen, energetic, tireless. But he refused to make use of cover. There was no crouching or crawling for Jan. He stood bolt upright. When it was pointed out to him that if he did that in a battle he would be killed, he answered simply that that was the duty of a junior officer. Otherwise he became a good mountaineer, a conscientious instructor.

One day I received the order that he was to return to his unit by a certain date. I passed it on through an orderly. When I next saw Jan there was a change in him. It was not that he looked either sad or heroic. He seemed greedy of the cheerful companionship which he had found. I was told that in a quiet moment he had said that he knew he was going to Cassino and he knew that he was going to be killed.

I said good-bye to him in the square with the P.U. truck which was to take him away ticking over only a few yards off. I thanked him for all his hard work, said how much we had liked having him with us, that I hoped to see him again soon—that sort of thing.

He did not answer at once. Then he said slowly, with an interval between each word, 'It has been home.'

He drew himself up and saluted—clean, stiff, smart, determined. But tears were streaming down his face. I had an urge to do something extravagant even though we were in public, to grasp him by the shoulders, put an arm round him. Instead I saluted and turned away.

I never saw him again.

7

The Mountain Warfare School

The visit to Cassino marked the end of a holiday. I picked up the trail again in the spring.

I followed the shore of the Lago di Barrea to the village of Barrea which is perched on a shelf above the water with a good view up the Sangro valley towards places where I had been. From the village the road twists and turns over a hill to the town of Alfedena. But the river goes there by a different route, through a deep gorge which it has cut out for itself. This is a much more interesting way. The T.C.I. guide says that it is practicable for those who do not suffer from vertigo, adding that it is 'ricca di orridi'—rich in precipices. It is certainly spectacular, but one is nowhere forced to take to the water so it does not come at the top of my list of gorges.

The river brings one back to the vicinity of the road just below Alfedena, a town which announces itself as 'Il Paese dei Dottori.'

It proved difficult to find out why. The local people shrugged their shoulders: no guide book gave the reason. Finally the mayor wrote to say that the phrase derived from a TV talk which had laid stress on the large number of professional men in Alfedena. In Italy lawyers, architects, economists, etc., all have university degrees—equivalent to our B.A. They are entitled to call themselves Dottore—and do. (The title is *not* exclusive to the medical profession and scientists.)

The mayor deplored the use of the phrase for publicity: he

thought it in doubtful taste. It would have been better, he said, to have given historical facts about Alfedena or mentioned its museum and natural beauties. The type in brackets below his signature showed him to be a Commendatore—about the equivalent to our C.B.E. He was not a Dottore.

From there my way parted from that of the Sangro, which I was sorry about as it is a fine river. I crossed a pass which is on the border of Molise, and came to the headwaters of the Vulturno. With the lofty Abruzzi left behind I was in a country of bumpy hills, many with villages balanced on top of them, and all I had to do was to walk rather a long way by twisting lanes to Isernia.

It was a day of April showers, and I did not have a mackintosh, so I took shelter where I could. First it was in a woodshed where one man was cutting logs with a motor chain saw while another watched him. The watcher and I exchanged greetings. Detecting my nationality he began in English a long description of his adventures in America and elsewhere. It was interesting, I think. But every few seconds the saw would bite into a log. The man's lips went on moving but I heard no more words until the screaming stopped. It is not quite accurate to say that Italians like noise. Rather they are unconscious of it.

When the next heavy shower came I was in a poor-looking and straggling village. I searched for the café, and found it; but it was shut for the lunch hour. So I sheltered in the porch and began eating what I had in my pack. The children were racing homewards from school. A very small boy, aged seven or eight, stopped, elbowed his way into the limited shelter of the porch, and stood with his head back, staring at my face as I pushed food into it. He did not look starving, and I was. I did not feel inclined to share my lunch with him—not that he asked for anything. He just stared, unblinkingly. It was embarrassing to eat with every mouthful being watched, worse than by a begging dog. At last I decided to try the power of the adult eye, and faced his stare with mine. So we remained for a good ten minutes with the rain splashing down a foot or two away. Then I could stand it no longer. 'What on earth do you want?' I burst out.

He fished in the pocket of his shorts, and brought out a 1,000-lira note. 'Can you change this?' he asked.

During the third shower I sheltered in a forge, and talked with the muscular blacksmith as well as I could against the *ping-pong-ping* of his hammer and the purr of bellows in the glowing coals. But the conversation did not matter. He was a beautiful workman, fascinating to watch.

I entered Isernia over a long and very high bridge over a torrent. The further bank of the deep, steep valley was terraced for houses and gardens of the town. I was halfway over the bridge when a Fiat *topolino* drew up some way in front. A small, dark man got out of it and unloaded a large full sack. With some difficulty he got it on the parapet of the bridge. I perked up for I have never seen a body dumped. But what came out of the sack was rags and paper. Nothing fell into the stream. A strong wind swept everything far and wide, to lodge eventually in trees and gardens and on house tops. The small, dark man carefully dusted and folded up the sack. He gave me a defiant look, then got into his *topolino* and drove away. That incident adequately suggests the character of Isernia.

Directly south and 10 miles distant from Isernia is the western end of the Monti di Matese, a remarkable and self-contained range about 25 miles long and 10 to 15 miles across, including the foothills. The peaks are between 3,000–4,000 feet in altitude, there is a lot of splendid woodland, varied by glens and pasture, and plenty of tumbling streams as clear—above the fringing villages—as the burns of the Scottish Highlands. I consider this little-known area of moderately high mountains and their foothills the most pastorally interesting and charming in all Italy. There are good grounds for this. The T.C.I. guide says, in translation: 'The Matese is one of the most important limestone massifs of the Italian peninsula, be it for its extent (over 1,000 square kilometres), its altitude (2,050 metres in Monte Miletto) or its richness in running water.'

It goes on to say that the fauna has been much reduced since the bandits killed off the bears. The wild boars and roe deer have become rare. But there are still plenty of wolves, foxes, hares, weasels, martens, badgers, wild cats and squirrels. Eagles still nest on the cliffs of Miletto, Gallinola and Tre Finestre. And there are many other birds of prey. In the lakes there are tench and in the rivers trout. The flora is rich.

I feel bound to quote these facts, for my experience of the Matese dates from the war when there was little time for nature study—though I am reminded of a senior officer who was with difficulty restrained from getting himself killed or captured by running wild in pursuit of a red admiral.

This I can say. The Matese are not wild in the *sauvage* sense as are some other parts of the Apennines. Much as I like the Gran Sasso and Maiella, for instance, I would hate to sleep out on them. They lack that element of kindliness. But I have often slept out on the Matese, under the beech trees by a stream or even in a snow shelter; and some of those nights I remember with pleasure.

So I looked forward keenly to seeing the mountains of Matese again. But the country between Isernia and the foothills was dull to say the best of it, and I was glad when a van driver stopped and offered me a lift. He was a dreamy-looking person. He leaned back in his seat with half-closed eyes as if on the point of falling asleep. None the less, he drove most of the time at between 60 and 70 m.p.h.—over 100 on his kilometre speedometer. Meanwhile he talked in a slow abstracted manner.

Having established my nationality and that I was on the way to visit friends at Sepino (this was actually true) he remarked that he had never learned English.

'You can have had little opportunity,' I said.

'Scusi, I have had every opportunity,' he answered. And then after a pause of half a minute—or more than half a mile—he added, 'I returned from Canada last October.'

I asked how long he had been there.

'Two months. I went with my family and we spoke only Italian.'

I enquired why he had returned so soon.

'We are not habituated to that climate,' he said.

I remarked that although Italy was delightful in spring and summer, winter in the Apennines could be rough. What made the Canadian climate intolerable in autumn?

'It is different,' he answered. 'Non siamo abituati.'

'But was it not very expensive going all that way with your family by ship?' I asked.

'By ship? We went by air. It cost me 500,000 lire'—about £340.

'That was a lot of money to discover that you did not like Canada,' I said.

He drove a mile in thoughtful silence, then said, 'It is not completely a bad country . . . I liked the cigarettes.'

This conversation had carried us round the western end of the Matese to the southern slopes. His intention was helpful because if my only wish had been to re-visit Sepino (on the northern rim of the range) he would be leaving me to walk over the shorter axis. It would have been difficult to convince him that I would have preferred to walk the length of the range. Besides, one must pay something for a lift—at least a show of interest in the driver's troubles.

He put me down at Alife and went racing off while I was still saying thank you.

From there I walked the few miles north to Piedimonte d'Alife, which as the name implies is at the foot of the mountains, here steep and sudden. I put up in the new albergo (I forget the name but it is the only one) where the pleasant young *padrona* gave me a good room with a private wash place and a tiny balcony overlooking a garden with a lemon tree in full fruit—for less than one pound.

It was then too late for lunch even in elastic Italy so I went out and bought a *panino* which I ate in my room. It was delightfully crisp, so much so that I broke two front teeth on it. This was as silly an accident as when, years previously, I had tried while climbing a hill to push down one of those smart socks which keep themselves up by elasticity and had broken a finger. I would not mention the teeth except that the lack of them had some significance later.

Next day I walked over the range from south to north. There was a new road which had almost been completed, and I kept to it most of the way. Except for short cuts, there was no practical alternative for when engineers survey for a road they find the best way. There were no difficulties apart from the climb and no hardship except on stretches where sharp stones had not yet been rolled in. I walked and walked, enjoying nostalgic views to either side. I was using an old wartime map which showed no road at all, and this roused the sentiments. There may be no justification for feeling regret for former lack of development, but I felt it just the same.

At the Lago di Matese, near the watershed, they had built an enormous new hotel. In spite of its beautiful site it appeared to be unoccupied, with only the litter of picnickers below its walls. Monte Miletto watched over the changing scene, snow-covered and impressive as ever.

It was while walking on, downhill now, that I came on the stretches of loose sharp stones and damaged one foot. It hurt so much that for a while I was doubtful of being able to reach Guardiaregia which would presumably be the first village on the new road. There was nobody about to ask, not a car—nothing. I took a daring short cut, dropping straight down a very steep hill. It came off, saving a couple of miles, and I limped optimistically towards Guardiaregia, content to leave Sepino, five miles on, for the morning.

Then I saw the head of the gorge of Guardiaregia at an angle to the smooth new road . . . In boyhood I often wondered about the meaning of the Old Testament phrase, 'his bowels yearned' for someone. I had since, of course, learned the importance of the bowels as a seat of feeling. In fear—of height particularly—one feels a pain there. But desire? . . . At that moment I had no subtle sentiment. I longed for the courage, strength and physical skill to force a way through that narrow corridor of swift water between sheer cliffs. I knew I had not these qualities and was scared to the bowels by the sight of the gulf. But I *had* been through it from top to bottom . . . One notices other people growing older. One now and then remarks on this in a kindly and sympathetic way. But rarely does one notice with the keenness of shock how much older one has grown oneself.

I did then. Never mind my feelings. I am describing the Apennines and the gorge of Guardiaregia is in my experience the most spectacular—and least known. A personal passage through it must be described, and the reader must excuse it being twenty-eight years old. I did it on a day off duty under the leadership of our unit doctor, Captain James Joyce, M.C., an experienced and skilful mountaineer. I wrote a diary account of it from which I quote. I do not think it is exaggerated. At the time it seemed no great achievement, only a stimulating outing.

*   *   *

It was a warm summer afternoon. James Joyce and I were dressed only in shorts and gym shoes, and carried a 100-foot length of alpine line.

The gorge formed gradually, so there was no difficulty about getting into it. We walked downstream in bright sunlight. But the rock walls grew steadily higher and closer together as if hinging on the stream. The water ran swiftly. It had gouged out a series of pools, deep and smooth-sided and curving inwards overhead. It was impossible to climb round these, so we swam them.

This first stage lasted for about half an hour. Then the noise of water increased, and we found ourselves standing on the lip of a waterfall some fifteen feet high. The stream was low after a period of fine weather. This had made swimming safe and easy so far, but at the same time it kept us down among the water-polished rock. It was impossible to climb round or down beside the falling water.

It was mainly for this sort of obstacle that we had brought the rope. James unwound it, doubled it, and hooked the middle over a projecting rock and threw the free ends down the fall. As every climber knows one can go down a rope like this without any difficulty at all by winding it round one's shoulders and between one's legs. When clad, this is perfectly comfortable. But the rope puckered up and seared my naked skin, so I tried to go down it hand over hand. An alpine line is thin as one's little finger. It slipped though my hands and I splashed into the pool.

When I had swum to the lower end I saw James following me, towing the rope by one end so that it ran round the projecting rock and finally came free. While he re-wound the coil we stood on a bed of shingle and looked back up the pool. It was evident that the waterfall was unclimbable. 'We are committed,' James said.

14. The Commonwealth Cemetery, Cassino. The rebuilt monastery on the hilltop behind.

15. The Matesa mountains from the plain to the north.

16. Le Tre Fontane, Sepino. The old water trough which now provides the water for a spa.

The sun was shining on the rocks five hundred feet above our heads, but at the bottom of the gorge it was dim and cool. Going on, we kept out of the water as much as we could, for each immersion was chillier than the last, and wet gym shoes slipped on the rock. Sometimes the gorge widened to twenty yards or so. Then we could scramble over the big boulders beside the stream. We did this with extreme caution, for although it was not difficult it was ideal terrain for spraining an ankle. Occasionally it was possible to traverse along the cliff edge of a pool. But before we or our shoes were really dry we were sure to be forced back into the water—knee deep, waist deep or swimming. More than once the gorge became so narrow, a mere cleft, that we had to swim dog-stroke. But in these cases the current was swift and for a short time we moved fast.

Some way further on the walls touched overhead. We swam with a powerful current and in almost complete darkness, wondering what was coming next. It would not have been possible to stop, for the walls offered nothing one could hold on to. This proved no worse than a test of nerves—in which I did badly. As we emerged from the tunnel there was a machine-gun *rat-tat-tat-tat* which sent me under water, although the noise was made by the metallic wings of a pigeon.

There followed several more waterfalls which we descended with the doubled rope. Then the gradient fell off and the water flowed more slowly. The surfaces of the pools were covered with insects and their bottoms were slimy. A black snake about a yard long swam across one of these pools, its head held high and its body undulating horizontally. We met no other snakes in the water but saw two small brown ones among the rocks.

The worst pool was one which seemed stagnant. It was covered by a thick brown scum. Swimming, one felt like an insect trying to push through the skin of cold boiled milk. The stink was abominable. It was a large pool, its lower end dammed by a big tree trunk which must have fallen long ago from high above. I reached it first and tried to climb out. But the trunk was too wide to get an arm over, and its surface was slimy with fungus. James tried to climb out over my shoulders. All that happened was that I was pushed under. Treading water, we looked round for an alternative way. But the pot-hole walls were smooth.

There was a splash, and James disappeared. I could not see him through the scum. Half a minute later he reappeared above the tree trunk which he had swum under. He leaned down and helped me up.

We were both very cold, shivering violently. All the time we had been able to see the sun shining on the northern canyon wall several hundred feet above. But we had always been in shadow or semi-darkness. Below the scummy pool the gorge curved, and in front of us we saw the sun shining on both walls. That meant that it must reach to the bottom. With a shout of excitement we hurried on.

The sunshine reached to the bottom of the gorge, but only in a canal-like stretch throughout which we had to swim until there was another curve and we were in shadow again.

That was not quite the end of it, however. In the course of the curve we saw a ledge fifty feet above, onto which the sunlight was pouring. There was no possible advance beyond that ledge but we climbed up to it and lay there, luxuriating in the warmth. Being comfortable, we appreciated the wild beauty of the scene—the tremendous walls of rock which swept up to the blue of the sky, the strange deep cleft which was an isolated world of shadow, water, reptiles and insects ... The sun moved on and left us in shadow again.

It needed moral as well as physical effort to climb down to stream level again and continue our advance. There were other waterfalls down which we had to rappel if we could not climb, other pools through which we swam or above which we climbed on mantelshelf ridges. Only one stands out. Because the water was very deep and therefore slow-moving, or because evening was coming on, the surface was black with mosquitoes. Swimming it wearily I got a mouthful.

Beyond, there was a sequence of caves and grottoes, eerie with bats. Here it was dream swimming, nightmare climbing.

Then we came to a pool of more than the usual length. It curved out of sight between smooth walls, in deep shadow. It would generally have been impossible to climb back up the water-fall cliffs we had descended. Now it came into both our minds that we might not be able to climb out of the lower end of this pool. Nothing was said at once, but James looked up and for a long time studied the cliffs above.

'Will it go?' I asked.

'It's possible. Are you game?'

With clumsy cold fingers we tied on the rope. Then James began to climb. The first pitch was very difficult and took him a long time, while I shivered below, my neck stiff from looking up. Then he reached the first finger-thin sapling, used it as a belay, and called me after him. It took me even longer than it had him, slipping in my wet gym shoes.

When I reached him he climbed on, leaving me secured to the sapling. Above the first pitch of polished stone the rock was friable, made of loose flakes the size of a coin and with inch-deep, outward-sloping ledges. A few tiny trees grew where their seeds had fallen, but it was all they could do to keep themselves up. There was nothing else to hold on to. While James climbed, his hands flat for maximum friction, a cannonade of stone flakes fell on me.

I made no notes about that climb except that we spent an hour on it. From below it had looked as if the slope eased off higher up, but experience did not bear this out. It was the nastiest sort of climbing, by friction and balance, with no secure holds. This is particularly exacting when you are tired. You can never relax for a moment. We were on a steep, unstable slope which ended on the lip of the final sheer cliff of water-polished rock. Above, the veritable trees began; but anything with roots worth the name was still several hundred feet higher up, possibly because that was the sun level.

I was the first to suggest turning back.

'I don't like changing a plan,' James said.

'This is too dangerous,' I said. 'It isn't climbing. It's gambling.'

He agreed. But then, looking down into the chasm, it was I who raised an objection.

'We could not reach the same trees with the doubled rope.'

James pulled out the sapling to which we were attached. 'Does it matter?' he asked.

We got back to the bottom of the gorge, swam the long, curving pool and scrambled out of its lower end without difficulty. But by now the light was fading. The old series of waterfalls, pools to swim or pools to scramble round continued, it seemed endlessly. I clearly remember one. There was a bigger drop than usual, and although it looked fairly easy to climb down I was too tired to be bothered. I held my nose and jumped.

At the lower end of the pool James turned on me furiously. 'That was a crazy thing to do. There might have been a rock just under the surface.'

'However, there was not,' I said.

'It's when you are tired that you take risks,' he went on. 'It's not courage, it's just bloody wrong. When you are tired you have got to be particularly careful.'

We were both drunk with weariness. There was no way of

knowing how much further the gorge continued, or what it held in store. Evening was falling fast. The thought of being benighted in that savage place, naked, cold and hungry, was terrifying.

In fact, we were almost at the end of our trials. The rock walls fell away like arms opening in welcome. The river looked as innocent as a babbling brook, not one which had sliced its way through a couple of thousand feet of mountain. We left it, and climbed back to the surface of the world. On the outskirts of Guardiaregia we found a patient driver waiting in a jeep. The passage of the gorge had taken us five hours. It cannot be more than a couple of miles long.

* * *

On the evening of the day I was describing before this reminiscence I limped into Guardiaregia. The new road has not yet enriched the village. It looked as it had when I last saw it—and probably as it had looked a century before. Its streets were almost deserted. I saw two men talking and said good evening to them.

'Buona sera, Signore,' they responded, taking off their hats.

'Can you please direct me to an inn?' I asked.

One of the men smiled slightly, sadly. 'The albergo is little and old, but —' He beckoned to a boy who was sitting on a doorstep. 'The ragazzo will guide you.'

The boy led me to a building which might have been a prison. It was made of stone and had a large iron-studded door. Having knocked I was admitted into the gloom and distinguished an old man, a young man with his hat on the side of his head, and a girl who reminded me of a suet pudding.

The old man was evidently the *padrone,* and I asked him for a meal and a bed. He did not understand. A certain type of person, once he realizes you are a foreigner, is convinced that he will not understand you, so he does not. The young man who was evidently a commercial traveller repeated my request in almost the same words. The *padrone* understood him and looked alarmed. He whispered something to the fat girl who led me into the dining room where such tables as had been used were still covered with morsels of bread. She told me to wait.

I waited an hour. It was growing dark and cold. I knocked on a glass door through which a light was glowing. The fat girl confronted me and told me to wait 'un momento'. After more than a moment I entered the lighted room. The *padrone,* his mother, his wife and the fat daughter were sitting in chairs watching a youngish man who was white with flour and was baking bread, pushing the dough into an oven with a thing like a wooden spade six feet long. On my entreaty he interrupted what he was doing to conduct me up stone stairs, along a stone floor corridor to a room with a bed in it, no more. He said he would make up the bed when he had finished baking, and then he would cook my supper. If I wanted to wash the place was in the garden. I asked if the fat girl couldn't do something about the bed and the supper, but he only shrugged his shoulders and hurried back to his baking.

Eventually he cooked a meal and served me. Later, while he was clearing away, we talked. He was an orphan who had lived with the family most of his life. He did all the domestic chores, cleaning and cooking, and also baked for the whole village. He was in effect the slave of the family who did not a stroke. I asked him if he remembered the war, and he said at once, 'Yes, I was hungry.'

Guardiaregia was as primitive a village as I had seen, but a passable hotel and a bit of tidying up could transform it into a resort very quickly. No doubt that will happen. It is in a splendid position.

I walked on towards Sepino feeling hungry and scrubby. I carried in my pack a baby immersion heater with the help of which I made morning coffee. I also had an electric razor with various adapters. Previously I had always been able to plug this in. But there had been no point in my room and the only electric light bulb was so high on the lofty ceiling that I had been unable to reach it even when I procured a chair and put it on the bed. So I had not shaved and, since it was freezing, had done a minimum of washing.

After walking an hour I stopped for breakfast of new bread, gorgonzola and wine. There were violets at my feet, the sun was shining and a lark was singing in the cloudless sky. Morale improved, and I remembered when I had first been this way. It was shortly after we had set up the mountain school at Sepino in 1943. A batch of young officers were brought out of the line to attend the first course. We worked them fairly hard, but they evidently felt that this was a wonderful welfare lark, and one night they beat up the village.

The Adjutant was much concerned. He said I would have to impose such severe punishments that word of it would get around and future students would arrive with a proper sense of awe. But one does not feel inclined to punish, or not by formal means, men who have been over-boisterous in an interval from fighting. I called them together and said that their behaviour showed they had not been working hard enough and had energy to spare. Therefore I would lead them on a training march.

We set off early next morning with full equipment, less ammunition. I did not at that time know the country at all well, so decided on following a rectangular course which should, mathematically, bring us back to Sepino. We went straight up into the mountains. We then turned right and followed the height of land until we reached the River Biferno. Here we again turned right and followed the river down to Guardiaregia though avoiding the gorge. The last lap of the walk was back to Sepino (I hoped) along the line that I was following on this day of reminiscence. But in

1943 there was no road, only a meandering mule track. These are abominable things even by daylight, for they are strewn with stones from the size of a ping-pong ball to that of a fist, and they roll beneath your feet. By night (it was by then dark) they express the nasty-mindedness of inanimate objects by hurting your toes and trying to sprain your ankles. We stumbled on, the leader uncertain of the way and hoping that nobody suspected this.

There was in the party a young New Zealander whose hair was so fair that it was almost white. On the occasion of the trouble he had made the night hideous with a song of which I remember the refrain:

> Caviar comes from the virgin sturgeon,
> Virgin sturgeon's a very fine fish.
> The virgin sturgeon needs no urgin',
> That's why caviar is my dish.

He still sang snatches now and then—a little flat. But apart from mutterings everyone else was silent.

We stumbled into Sepino shortly before midnight. The Adjutant, who had not been on the march, viewed the struggling band with satisfaction. 'You'll have no more trouble, sir,' he said brightly. 'The C.O. leading the punitive exercise—this will get around. You did just the right thing, sir.'

But I had already received an utterly sincere compliment. In the darkness behind me a voice had muttered, 'If I had a round in this rifle I'd shoot that bloody man Scott.'

That bloody man became a dictator to the civil population. For instance, Sepino was an extremely picturesque mountain village, with steep cobbled streets over which the tightly packed houses here and there met to form an arch. But there was no sanitation. The householders used to slip out of their doors in the morning, do what they had to do in the street, and slip back again. Consequently the place stank and was insanitary. I instituted a morning patrol of *carabinieri* and one British soldier. If human excreta was found the nearest house was fined 1,000 lire on the spot. There may well have been a certain amount of dumping, but it worked. With the money we hired road sweepers and built loos.

Once we gave a ball. The irrepressible adjutant, Ken Kettle, sent out the invitations, 'His Excellency the Grand Colonel Commandant-in-Chief requests the pleasure . . .' It was taken seriously and I was thereafter addressed as Eccellenza.

All that had been twenty-six years before. And now I was going back. An Italian colonello is an essentially respectable person. Here was I in creased and muddy clothes, with two front teeth missing, unshaven and carrying a pack—a *barbone,* a tramp to all appearances. I almost turned aside at the last moment. But I very much wanted to see the place again, and I was sure that I would not be recognized. I would have a look round and then continue on my way.

Having located my house, the office, the mess and so on I went to the café on the piazza for a beer. It was noon and a number of men were sitting or standing about. They stared fixedly at me, but that is not unusual in a small village.

'Are you not Colonello Scott?'

Three oldish men had approached, and challenged me. When I admitted the charge there was a shout and everyone in sight was brought into the huddle to be given a colourful résumé of the British occupation.

'Do you remember me?' one man demanded.

'Yes,' I lied. 'But how clever of you to remember me.'

'How should I forget you?' he demanded in what sounded an angry tone. He spun round and addressed the audience. 'My son was bitten by a mad dog. The doctor said that he would die unless he was taken at once to the hospital in Naples. There was no transport, none. I went to the colonello.' He turned on me again. 'What did you do?'

I shook my head for I did not remember.

He turned his back on me and continued speaking in a voice charged with emotion. 'The colonello at once put a military camion at my disposal, with a driver and escort. My son was rushed to Naples and his life was saved. Does one forget a thing like that? In Italy we forget evil—there is so much. But a good deed, never!'

So it went on, reminiscence capping reminiscence, questions about the other officers. I was put in a car and driven round. I was taken to the Tre Fontane just outside the village. This used to be a simple mule trough fountain where one drank when returning from the mountains. A scientist had discovered that the water contained minerals beneficial to some organ or other. Now they were building an establishment over it and the place would become a spa. Hundreds, I was told, already come to Sepino on holiday. Soon thousands would come for their health. Poor old Sepino!

I was given lunch—heaven knows what else. At last I got away. I had not gone three miles before a car came racing after me. A brisk little man jumped out and wrung my hand.

'I was away at Campobasso. When I returned to Sepino I heard that you had been there. I had to see you,' he said. His eyes were dancing. 'Do you remember the fire?'

I did. A fire among old, tightly packed houses has very serious possibilities. There was no fire brigade nearer than Campobasso, over fifteen miles away, and no telephone link. So the troops were turned out and we had a carnival, climbing ladders, smashing through windows, sloshing water about, scrambling over the tiles. I remembered it as a tremendous spree.

'You were wounded,' said my old friend, 'in the leg, no the arm. You were streaming with blood. But you still led the assault ... And do you remember what you said to the commander of the fire brigade which arrived when it was all over?'

Excited by strain, I had dared to be rude to an official in uniform, something which to an Italian seems the height of courage.

I walked on finally, not a sadder but a wiser man. 'The evil that men do lives after them.' How wrong that is! Do just one thing worth praise and it is remembered for ever—at least in Italy.

8

Lacrima Christi

As you walk southward from Sepino the Matese mountains shrink and flatten out. There is nothing left of them by the time you leave Molise and enter Campania. This latter is a varied Region, containing Naples, Vesuvius, the spectacular peninsula of Sorrento, some bald mountains, and the horticultural land of Campania Felix.

In the northern part of Campania, which I had just entered, the Apennines take a rest. They are still there, of course, but they are, so to speak, lying down. It would have been an uninspiring walk to Benevento except that the blackthorn—which the Italians call *biancospino*—was in flower, and the fruit trees in blossom. The Italian *primavera* is shorter than the English spring, but it is vigorous and colourful.

Benevento is a guide-book town. Except by its Arch of Trajan I was not greatly impressed. It is an untidy place with every little-used corner strewn with litter. I had become highly reactive to litter since passing the new hotel by Lago di Matese and seeing an otherwise pretty area thickly strewn with rubbish presumably thrown from picnickers' cars. We in Britain have little right to cast the first bottle at a litterer, but there are some interesting points about the vice.

The amount of litter in a country is in inverse proportion to its latitude. In Scandinavia there is none. By the time one moves south to Britain there is already quite a lot—too much. In France it is worse, in Italy worse still. This last is strange, for the Italian has a passion for orderliness: consider the exactly arranged piles of fruit in a greengrocer's window. But outside their own premises the world is their dustbin.

Most of this rubbish—tin, glass, plastic, greaseproof paper—is indestructible by natural means. Therefore it will grow, will spread from the beauty spots to the ugly places. Europe will become buried by litter as much of it once was by ice. But the Rubbish Age will differ from the Ice Age in that it will spread from the south northward. Wait a hundred years and see if I am not right.

This book has shown a certain interest in names. That of Benevento is intriguing. The town was founded either by Diomedes (whom I knew nothing about until I looked him up in an encyclopaedia) or—as I prefer to believe—by the illegitimate son of Ulysses and Circe. He, disgruntled, called it Malventum—although why a Greek should use Latin I don't know. The ill wind blew nobody any good until the Romans made the place a colony in 268 B.C. and changed its name to Beneventum. So simple and sensible! Benevento was the scene of a bloody battle which is in all the prefaces to Dante because it was fought just before his birth and altered the political scene in Italy. Benevento was also, briefly and unsuccessfully, a principality which Napoleon in his grand way gave to Talleyrand. So the town is not associated with any great success. But the new name appeased superstition.

Italians are superstitious. The most remarkable sight I saw in Benevento was a black cat. They are virtually extinct in Italy: I suppose they are drowned as kittens. But here was a black cat strutting about with its tail in the air, entirely inconsiderate of anyone to whom it brought bad luck by crossing his path.

I witnessed another remarkable incident at Benevento. Walking along a pavement I approached a blind beggar who sat cross-legged beside an upturned hat in which were a number of coins. A woman in a fur coat dropped into the hat a hundred-lira piece (worth about 13 pence) then scrupulously picked out ninety lire in small change. I felt that Christ would have been inspired to a good parable by that.

Currently, a Benevento firm produces Strega, which means witch and is a popular sticky liqueur, something like a yellow Chartreuse. During the war they made what they called gin but which a distiller in uniform told me was nearer to a not bad whisky. At any rate it was strong. The Canadian Division sent a water truck to collect their requirement.

I spent two nights in Benevento to rest my poor feet, and occupied the day between by a bus journey along the Via Appia to visit the Caudine Forks, which are said to be a defile near Boiano, some fifteen miles to the west. Ancient battlefields are rarely satisfactory. I could not see how a Roman army could have got itself trapped here between barricades of tree-trunks and boulders.

Back in my hotel room I unfolded the map on the floor and drew a ruler line from Benevento to Eboli, which seemed a good place to stop. Next morning I set out to follow it. I walked along the banks of the River Sabato which flowed close to my line. The valley was flat-bottomed but it was not too wide. It was wooded and it narrowed as one went upstream, with quite formidable mountains to either side. All the fruit trees were in blossom, splashes of pink or white on a green background. Vines, still naked, were trained between trees and posts. They looked like snakes twenty or even thirty yards long. There were big groves of hazels, presumably grown for the nuts. There were intensely cultivated patches of vegetables. But I wondered why Campania was ever called Felix—inland from its beautiful coast. The soil (here and elsewhere) looked fertile, but the peasants looked almost desperately poor—which can only mean that they got no more than a bare living from the land. Possibly they work it on the *mezzadria* principle by which half of all the produce goes to the landlord. But here I was in the spring, with the countryside burgeoning, and almost every human being I saw was wretchedly dressed and bent double over the toil of the field. One hears much talk about the idle Neapolitans. But in the country, by God, they work. It made me feel guilty to be able to stroll along doing nothing for my livelihood, only enjoying myself.

I reached Atrepalda, a long, unbeautiful village which merges into Avellino. There was accommodation of a sort. Then in front of me there was a long stretch with very little on the map, something of an empty quarter covered by the extended name of Monti Picentini. It proved pleasurably empty on the ground: a good finishing stretch to Eboli. It was too far to cover in a day, and I got the best that I could hope for—a rough roof over a hard bed. But it was an excellent walk. From Atrepalda a minor road took me almost due south to Santa Lucia di Serino and then to plain Serino. Here the road curves south-westward to go to Salerno, so I left it and took as guide the head waters of my old friend the River Sabato. There was a track, unmetalled and remarkably untravelled, to Curti and Giffoni, and thence to Montecorvino which is comparatively large, though only a village. There were good mountains to both sides, particularly on my left (the east), but the way was never hard.

The map showed no track on to Eboli without a wide detour. In fact a new unmetalled road zigzags up and down laboriously. I went straight up into the downs—for the last ridge before Eboli is like the downs. I picnicked on the top beside a ruined house and had a memorable meal. Behind was the way I had come, always a pleasure in retrospect. In front was the great Salerno plain, patchworked with cultivation. The sea gave a straight base to the triangle. The other two sides were formed by mountains which

17.   Vesuvius—the cone of the 1944 eruption, a general aerial view.

18.   Vesuvius seen from the outer crater, 1944.

19. National costumes: (a) Tiriolo, (b) the Albanian villages of Calabria, (c) Scanno in the Abruzzi.

rose steeply from the flat. If the sea rose only a few feet the plain would be a wide bay. Directly below me was Eboli. It was not anything very remarkable to look at, but it was the end of my road for the present, and that means something. Carlo Levi, a Jew, was interned there by the Fascists during the war, and the place inspired his well known novel, *Cristo si è fermato a Eboli*. It is depicted as a place of unredeemed squalor.

I walked down to it through olive groves. On a track I met a large flock preceded by half a dozen dogs which made a show of attacking me and then went on. The sheep passed silently, busily, seemingly endlessly. The shepherd, who came last, raised his hat.

Eboli straggles up the hill, and as I strode down automatically after the long distance I had walked I had the strange impression that I was stationary, and that the buildings were passing me in procession. In Italy generally, in Apennine towns and villages certainly, the church comes first in social respect and architectural importance. Appropriately, the Basilica di San Pietro alli Marmi led this procession, a fine old thing. Then, incongruously, came a new church with glaring stained-glass windows. Then, incongruously, followed the houses of the old town hand in hand, dilapidated dwellings with balconies crowded with flower pots, set along paved streets, passages, stairways—for the way was still steep. Next came relics of a town wall with plants growing between the stones ... A tradesman's three-wheeled van struggled upwards, blaring jazz music and sales talk from trumpets on its top. Then there was a house with a plaque boasting that it gave hospitality to Garibaldi in 1860. That too seemed an anachronism, the date was so recent. But on its heels came the new town—of the last few years but already shabby—a barracks of a school, a ten-storey block of flats, cars hooting urgently, the town clock which had stopped at half past four.

But the piazza made up for this. It was ageless. A funeral was in progress outside a church in one corner, busy market-stall selling in another. And the memorial to the first world war had a touch which moved me. It was a statue group of soldiers, idealized certainly; but it had been shot up in the second war—for Eboli was the apex of the bridgehead of the Salerno landing. The marble of the centrepiece was blistered. The dying bronze soldier had received a real bullet through the chest.

Vesuvius is on the western edge of the Apennines, but not a part of them. They are the result of an upheaval which was finished and done with before man appeared upon the Earth, and their dead rocks will never change except by the infinitely slow process of erosion. The volcano is alive today and still growing, occasionally piling up more ash and lava. At other times it smokes its pipe of apparent peace. But this graceful plume of smoke is a reminder of the fantastic forces which are beneath our feet, sufficiently close to the surface hereabouts to express themselves in eruptions and earthquakes. Italy has not yet made peace with the Devil who is armed with molten rock and poison gas. It was probably the latter which knocked out the people of Pompeii and Herculaneum in A.D. 79 before the ashes buried them.

The intense drama of that catastrophe has stolen the thunder of those which have happened since—in the years 472, 685, 1036, 1139, 1500 and 1631, for instance. The latest eruption of notable size was in 1944. This I was lucky enough to see. By night it looked like all the fireworks displays that there have ever been rolled into one. By day there was an immense dark cloud illuminated from below, the colour of blood. Lava flowed down the mountainside as slowly as thick treacle. You could leave a penny to be engulfed, and hook it out burnt to an extraordinary colour. Every living thing in the path of the lava was totally destroyed, and—as the molten rock solidified—encased in armour. The feeling that this unhurried treacle flow gave one was of utter helplessness.

There were interesting minor phenomena. Quantities of fine red dust were thrown high into the atmosphere. An officer stationed far from Naples had been relaxing with a bottle of whisky and went out to see that it was raining blood. He told me that the effect was sobering. Dust from Vesuvius has been recorded in Turkey and North Africa. It may well be carried much further.

With the possible exception of the Matterhorn, Vesuvius is the most photogenic mountain. As I started homewards from Eboli it occurred to me that there exist innumerable pictures of Vesuvius as seen from the Bay of Naples, but as far as I knew none of the Bay of Naples as seen from Vesuvius. I wanted to have that view.

Monte Somma (the Mons Summanus of the Romans) is the proper name of the mountain as a whole, Vesuvius applying only to the present volcanic cone. Etna and Fujiyama are perfect cones. As seen from Naples, Mount Somma appears to approach that shape. In fact it is a great circular girdle of cliffs, separated from the eruptive cone, the remains of a far greater crater of more ancient date. The valley between the active cone and the relic of original crater wall is called Atrio di Cavallo. The altitude of the highest point varies. It is about 4,000 feet. As has been said it tends to grow, but it may blow its top off.

There is no difficulty about the climb. If you cannot get transport it is just a slog up a road which reaches to within 1,000 feet of the top. This need not be dull, however. Although obvious when you have thought about it, it is intriguing to find that any liquid—not only water but also liquid rock—follows the easiest course. Thus you see glaciers of lava, streams of it solidified in gullies. And you note the first vegetation to grow as soon as fallen dust has provided roothold and nourishment. Of the bigger things, fir trees and broom appear. But there are pioneer colonies of lesser plants. The housing problem is even more urgent in the vegetable kingdom than in the human.

Above the roadhead you climb a zigzag path cut out of the cinder slope. I was wearing a pair of oldish but still quite respectable shoes which I had kept to go home in. This path and what followed ruined them entirely.

Vesuvius is well organized. As you approach the rim you are required to pay 260 lire. I vocally surmised that this was tribute to the Devil. But money is needed to maintain the path, also to pay guides and officials above. Being undisciplined, I climbed onto a tufa eminence. I was at once called down, and tardily obeyed. Later it was explained to me, quietly and politely, that the lump I had scrambled up was liable to collapse into the crater at any moment. I was impressed. The living volcano has moods and weaknesses of which those placed in charge are aware. Without surveillance a number of people would no doubt kill themselves.

The crater is a good 1,000 feet deep, ending in the plug which will be blown out by the next eruption. You see no molten rock as you may in Etna, but smoke oozes out of the bottom of this vast devil's punchbowl, and there is a strong smell of sulphur. I saw a priest walking slowly round the rim, his head bent, reading his breviary while the hellish fumes curled up around him. While I watched him he did not once raise his eyes from the page. He might by his behaviour have been in the cloisters of a cathedral. Yet he must have climbed to this high place for some specific reason.

All sorts of other people were scrambling along the path which capped the crater rim—broken battlements of basalt and slopes of ash. Most were parties under the tenuous hold of a guide. Some were families with children. There was even a dachshund waddling imperturbably along. But, alone or among crowds, Vesuvius is impressive to the impressionable. Walking down I felt close to understanding the priest's motives. In a place like this one comes nearest to experiencing Heaven and Hell as our ancestors believed them to be.

The slopes of Vesuvius below the basalt and lava line are probably the most fertile in Italy. The volcanic dust is extremely rich in ingredients which promote vegetable growth. One has heard that moon soil has similar qualities. Is this a practical expression of the Phoenix myth—life from ashes? At least it is true that the slopes of Vesuvius, although well known for centuries to be dangerous, are thickly populated by people who work the exceptionally good soil. The reward makes the risk worth while. If one could believe in an unbenign Providence one could see Vesuvius as a baited trap.

One wonders if this is connected with the evocative name of the local wine, Lacrima Christi? There is, in books and brochures, a legend about the origin of the name. When Satan was thrown from Heaven he tore out a patch of Paradise as he fell. He came to earth on the slopes of Vesuvius. Later, Christ visited the torn-out patch of Paradise and wept for the human sin and penury he saw. His tears watered a vine which thereafter produced 'the wine of the sad name which above all others makes the heart glad'.

A pretty legend, but one could not take it for more than that. I had drunk Lacrima Christi on several occasions—in Naples, in Salerno, in Rome, in London. I believe it is also exported to the United States. Only a few days previously I had drunk it at Atripaldo. On that occasion the label had given the wine its full name, Lacrima Christi di Vesuvio, but the producer was a firm in Atripaldo—which was not entirely satisfactory although the grapes could have been brought the fifty-odd miles from Vesuvius. In any case I wanted to see the vineyards, drink the genuine wine there, and if possible find a more satisfying origin of the name— the best wine name there is.

I knew that the wine may be either red or white; that the red is ruby red, dry, almost astringent, refreshing to the palate; that the white is amber coloured, slightly aromatic, and with a velvet smoothness in the mouth. (I am ignoring the wines of false pretences, grown Di'el knows where that no more fit the bottle labelled Lacrima Christi di Vesuvio than the glass slipper fitted the Ugly Sisters.) I had read in P. G. Garoglio's enormous and authoritative *Nuovo Trattato di Enologia* that the red is made of Aglianico, Piede di Palumbo and Soricella grapes on the eastern and southern slopes of Vesuvius; the white of Greco di Torre and Fiano grapes in the same area. The search seemed easy.

I went to Terzigno on the south-eastern slopes of the volcano. The village is so named because it has been thrice overwhelmed by an eruption. I had an introduction to a producer, but he was dead. So I went to a café, which is generally the best place to find things out. Everyone in Terzigno is in some way or other concerned with the making of wine, but it seems nobody drinks it. The café was empty and the barman knew nothing useful.

Then a young priest appeared and guided me to a wine factory which contained huge vats and the most modern equipment. But when I asked the proprietor if he made Lacrima Christi he laughed and said, 'There is no such thing—until wine finds itself in a bottle with that label.'

I protested; 'But all the authorities say that Lacrima Christi comes from this district.'

'From here!' The proprietor found that a splendid joke. 'Here the peasants are so mean that they will not prune their vines. Therefore their wine is plentiful but thin as vinegar. I import grapes from Benevento. They strengthen up the local wine.'

'What do you call the wine you make?' I asked.

'I don't call it anything. I sell it in bulk. Taste it. It is good and strong.'

It was strong.

The young priest, seeing my disappointment, took me to the church and introduced me to his *parroco*. The young priest was the curate. His *parroco,* the vicar, was a big, brown-complexioned, smiling, fearless-looking man. A number of youths had followed us into the precincts of the church; and they stood in a group about the *parroco,* their faces suddenly alight, talking with animation. In that poor village where there was no theatre, no cinema, scarcely a sign of comfort, the House of God rang with happy laughter.

When the *parroco* heard of my interest, and my recent experience, he looked at me thoughtfully with his straight brown eyes and said, 'I will give you wine of the district which is absolutely pure.'

I asked what it was.

'Our Communion wine,' he said.

I, a Presbyterian, drank it with reverence. It was a virgin wine, clean and young. It had a family likeness to the Lacrima Christi I knew. But it was too small, too innocent.

The *parroco* explained that at vintage time he sent a cart with a barrel on it round the vineyards. Each faithful parishioner dropped into the barrel a few of his best bunches, and from these the Communion wine was made in a shed outside the vestry door. The district was right, he said, the grapes were of the right sort. But the wine was as poor as the people who made it because they could not afford to feed the soil.

'If I had a grape I would show you,' he said. 'Crush one of these grapes and it drips water. But crush a grape from well tended soil —of the same district—and the drops are large and glistening as tears. From them the true Lacrima Christi is made.'

I asked him where I could find the vineyards which grew those grapes.

'Go to Boscotrecase,' he said.

Presumably this village once consisted of three houses in a wood. Now it is a long and straggling place. And my luck failed. I had not realized how fortunate I had been at Terzigno. Although I had not found what I was looking for, I had had an interesting experience, met pleasant people. Not that they were unpleasant in Boscotrecase: they seemed eager to help. But they could not quite understand what this strange foreigner was after.

Then from someone in the group that had gathered I heard reference to Pane-perso. Lost-bread was an unusual name for a person, and I asked for an explanation. I did not get one but was told how to find the person. He would help me if anybody could.

The place to which I was directed proved to be a small restaurant with quite a lot of cultivated land about it, high up on the southern side of Vesuvius, above the other houses. The scene was remarkable—on the one hand the steep cinder slopes of the volcano, on the other the smiling and sparkling Bay of Naples. But I did not appreciate it just then. I was tired, hot and thirsty. A vigorous-looking man of rather less than middle age was standing in the doorway and I asked if he was Pane-perso.

'So they call me,' he answered. 'What can I do for you?'

I told him that I wished to see the vineyards of the true Lacrima Christi and to drink the wine in the place where it was made.

Immediately and with confidence he led me down into a cellar hewn and blasted out of black basalt, which is solidified lava. The chambers were extensive as a catacomb, cool as dawn and lined with bottles and barrels. He took out a bottle, holding it so that I could see the label. I read:

Nuova Casa Bianca
LACRYMA CHRISTI
propr: Pasquale Vitulano
(Italia) Boscotrecase (Napoli)

'Is that what you are looking for?' he asked.

'It is spelt with a y, but, yes —' I said cautiously.

He drew the cork, filled a glass and gave it to me.

I held it under my nose, took a mouthful, chewed it slowly, swallowed.

'Is that the wine?' he asked.

I shook my head. 'No, it is better, much better.'

Italians are connoisseurs of compliments, and his eyes signalled the equivalent of 'I receive you loud and clear'. He pulled up two chairs, filled two glasses. Any white wine drunk in its own cellar, undisturbed and at the temperature in which it has grown up has an advantage. Any drink when you are in need of it is that much better. Scene plays its part in appreciation. But this wine at that moment was inspired. Whatever the experts say, tastes cannot be described except by comparisons, and to this there was none.

'The Tears of Christ, Lost-bread, Pasquale—of Easter, of death and resurrection . . .' I pondered aloud.

His dark, intelligent eyes were on my face.

'It was my father who was called Pane-perso,' he said, 'His baptismal name was the same as mine, Pasquale. I will tell you his story.'

It is artificial to pretend to repeat a tale in the speaker's words, and in any case I must translate. So I will record the facts as I remember them.

Pasquale Vitulano, the father, bought land above the other holdings. It was cheap, there was room, and the soil seemed very good. Working from dawn till dusk under the lazy smoke cloud of the volcano he created a farm—vineyards, olive groves, orchards of lemons and oranges, plots of vegetables, melons, pumpkins. He became prosperous. He had a fine house, a wife, and the beginnings of a large family.

Then came the eruption of 1906. This was of lava, not ashes. The lava welled over the crater rim and poured down like the boiling tar with which they surface roads, but of course infinitely hotter. It travelled fast over the steep upper slopes; then, as the gradient became less, it moved slowly, often seeming on the point of stopping. But more and more lava overflowed above, pouring over the lower layers, moving slowly, inexorably on.

While he watched helpless, the burning tide reached his vines and olives. They disappeared. His fruit trees went in a puff of smoke. His vegetable garden was buried. The lava crept on to the house, burned it and gradually engulfed the ruins. He and his young family retreated with what they could carry. But they had no money, for he had put everything into the farm.

When the eruption was over and he returned it was difficult to be certain even where the farm had been. Everything was buried under a metre or two of black rock. As far as the eye could see everything was black.

Vitulano, Pane-perso, set to work at once. He carried up earth and began to make a new layer of soil. What he first planted is interesting. He was near starving, but instead of something which would produce food he planted pines. They were of no practical value but, winter and summer, they relieved the black desolation.

Then he blasted through the lava and set vines in the still fertile ground below. He cut out a water cistern and the cellars already mentioned. He began the house which is now the Nuova Casa Bianca. He visited Pompeii and Herculaneum where the archaeologists were glad that he should carry away as many loads of *lapilli* as he would. These minute pumice pebbles, weathered by time, make excellent soil. He spread it over the lava to the depth of a metre, and grew in it all that he had grown before. He was a clever gardener whose crops were always larger than those of anybody else. Or perhaps it was just that he worked harder and with more care in cultivating his vegetables. But most of all he was devoted to his vines and to his trees—the fruit trees and the conifers which had first brought the relief of greenness to his eyes. He tended the vines, and when the wine was making he would sit up all night with it, taking the temperature of the fermenting juice, ensuring that it had enough air but not too much. And every day he visited his trees.

Vesuvius left him alone while his family of eight boys and girls grew up, married and had children of their own. In the Italian way most of them remained at home or set up house nearby. Pane-perso became a patriarch. But he remained strong, active and clear-minded.

One Sunday morning he came down, had his coffee, and then as his habit was set out on a tour of his land accompanied by a small grandson. He was away longer than usual, alone with the child on that day of rest. When he returned to the house he sat down in his big chair.

But the child's eyes were troubled. He was restless and seemed afraid. At last he told the women who were preparing lunch, 'Nonno was funny today.'

'Hush,' they said. 'He is resting.' And then of course they asked in what way his grandfather had been funny. The child answered that he had gone to every tree and patted it and said, 'Good-bye, old friend.'

'Don't be silly,' the grown-ups said. But the child's fear had infected them. They went to look at the old man, and found that he was dead.

Pane-perso, the son, led me out of the cool, dim cellar into the blazing sunshine, and took me on a tour of his land. It was an oasis of different greens—dark pines, glaucous olives, brilliant citrus trees, classic figs, sprouting vegetables. All these grew in a soft rich soil. But in places the lava lay bare, and here—through cracks which had been blasted in it—vines grew thick of stock and vigorous. Above this verdant scene the dark volcano stood, smoking peacefully.

'The eruption of 1944—did it affect you?' I asked.

'No, it stopped short,' he answered, and pointed to the place which the lava had reached. It was not far away.

9

A Detour from Eboli

From the apex of the triangular Salerno plain, a few miles inland from Eboli, the valley of the River Sele leads a road into the enfolding hills. Some ten miles further eastward the Sele is joined by a tributary almost as large as itself, the Tanagro. For both rivers there is a sharp change of direction near this junction, for the upper Sele flows from the north, the Tanagro from the south.

The Tanagro from its source at the head of the Vallo di Diano comes near to cutting off the lump of country to the westward which is already notched to north and south respectively by the Gulf of Salerno and the Gulf of Policastro. This lump of country—the term is anything but rude, referring to its mountainous character—is called the Cilento. It is now still more effectively cut off by the Autostrada del Sole. For that is what motor roads do. Certainly they connect big cities. But because one can only get on or off them here and there they effectively isolate the sparsely populated country in between.

In the case of the Cilento this is particularly striking. It has an old road which meanders through it fairly near the coast, turning inland and uphill at wonderful Paestum, wandering vaguely up to Vallo di Lucania, and finally coming down to Sapri at the head of the Gulf of Policastro—twenty miles or so from the Autostrada del Sole. Except on local journeys, who will any longer use the old road which takes three times as long as the autostrada?

I have not explored the Cilento, merely been through it by car.

So I only know it as a wild, well wooded, mountainous area with green valleys and some fine outcrops of rocks, with picturesque villages here and there. The coast is said to have many rocky harbours and little sandy bays. It cannot be crowded. People who say they have difficulty in finding solitude have not really tried.

In the summer following the last chapter I started from Eboli, and at the junction of the two rivers turned northward up the Sele. This was in anything but the direction of the Toe, of course. But I felt that I ought to get across the range to Monte Vulture because that is a hinge on which the Apennines change direction, much as they do at San Marino.

I did not stay long in the valley of the Sele, soon bearing eastward instead. This part of the Apennines is high, wide, and—on the whole—handsome, with as long views in all directions as you can find anywhere in the range. But it is not memorable. The mountainscape is too haphazard to be remembered in any detail. And the villages are all alike in their primitive simplicity. Rarely was there anything particular to catch the eye. If there were it was probably a ruin:

> A castle, precipice-encurled
> In a gash of the wind-grieved Apennine.

I walked a long way, I got very hot. My mind wandered. I find little in my diary about those days. Only a few uncomplimentary notes:

'A mass of mountains, some wooded, some bare, not ordered in pattern but surging up as undisciplined individuals. Can the Apennines have influenced the national character?' Later, reaching the middle line, I returned to the metaphor of a stormy sea. 'A tide race of tall hills, an after-storm ocean with a cross-swell.'

The first landmark of note was the great Norman castle which stood in bold silhouette against the evening sky above Melfi. As one approached, interest in this medieval scene increased—the town walls, the clustering old houses, the dominant castle. But close inspection proved less satisfactory. The dry moat of the castle was strewn with litter, the postern at that hour was closed, and one was faced by a large notice which stated in effect that this restored relic of the past came to one by courtesy of the Cassa per il Mezzogiorno with some assistance from the Normans. (The Cassa per il Mezzogiorno is the fund from the national exchequer —the Northerners say of Northern money—devoted to the development of the South: one sees signs of it all over the place from Naples downwards.) Interest in the town was soon exhausted as one wandered about the little streets, although the interest of the townspeople in the stranger with a pack remained lively.

Melfi is highly praised in guide books, and indeed it is a place of history. But I am not alone in my lack of wholehearted appreciation. I have at home a Baedeker of 1908. It says: 'The earthquake of 1851 completely ruined the town, since when it has been rebuilt without, however, improving its cleanliness.'

Melfi is in an earthquake zone. The foundations of the town wall are part of a subsidiary cone of the volcano called Monte Vulture, which is a few miles to the south. Vulture is extinct, but the only volcano alive or dead on the east side of the Apennines. It does not look its 4,365-foot altitude, for the cone rises from quite high ground. It is thickly wooded with oaks and noble beech trees, and on its summit is a radar tower which keeps watch on the Albanians. Of coincidental interest, Barile, below the volcano's eastern slopes, was settled by Albanians in the Middle Ages, and like all of the many Albanian villages in Italy retains some signs of its founders in language, customs or dress. There will be more to say about these settlements when we reach the thicker concentration of them further south.

Below the western slopes of Vulture and still among fine trees are the two pretty lakes of Monticchio. I slept in a scatter-brained inn on the shores of one of them. When I asked for a room the cook and/or proprietor insisted upon my tasting a *pizza* he had just made before he would answer my request. At supper I was waited on by a boy of twelve, a bouncing extrovert who talked more than he served. 'Is it true,' he asked, 'that the English eat four meals a day?' I told him that we eat three or four but in total less food than the Italians. 'I can see that,' he said. 'You are thin. Italians are fat. That is why we lost the war.' I wondered who or what had put that into his head.

The wines of the district deserve to be drunk, for they are unquestionably the best in all Basilicata. Here again is proof that volcanic soil is good for vines. There is a red Aglianico, a sweet and heavy Moscato Bianco and an amber-coloured Malvasia, which is a dessert wine. They are all 'del Vulture' and made respectively of Aglianico, Moscato and Malvasia grapes. These types are well known elsewhere, but those grown on Vulture possess the remarkable peculiarity that the wine made from them becomes fizzy entirely of its own accord within a couple of months of being bottled. Undoubtedly the bouncing boy had been brought up on this wine.

From Vulture I went south to Potenza, some thirty miles away, through rather undistinguished mountain country, quite high but so even that it seemed not to be. Halfway there was an oasis of great interest, Frederick II's splendid castle, Lagopesole. He built it for a hunting lodge, they say; but he must surely have had in mind the possibility of being hunted himself. The building gives a sense of enormous strength. It is four-square, with rounded towers at the corners and scarcely an outside window. What

20. Campania Felix.

21. The high Sila plateau: a north-European landscape in southern Italy.

did Frederick hunt? one wonders, looking at the naked hills. But in his time, the thirteenth century, they were covered with forest.

That is the general rule. The south of Italy was once thickly forested. The trees, as is their way, drew rain and sheltered the top-soil from the wind. Then absentee landlords had them felled to raise money. The rain, which then fell in occasional savage cloud-bursts, washed the fertile soil into the sea or left mud to dry into dust for the wind to deal with. Now the Corpo Forestale and other organizations, backed by Cassa per il Mezzogiorno money, are trying to put things right. But it is one thing to cut down trees and quite another to make them grow again.

A detachment of the Corpo Forestale was stationed in the castle. One man was drawing water from the medieval well. I dare say the mod. cons. are much as they were in Frederick's day. But the castle is all the better for a bit of life.

Potenza with its midi-skyscrapers is not a beauty. Due to earth-quakes and war, many of its houses are new and therefore—that being the tendency—ugly. But it greets one with 'Benvenuto' which is at least polite; better than 'Evitare rumori inutili'— which would be *inutile*. And the town offers accommodation, food and wine. I spoke just now of an oasis of interest. Of more importance, I'm afraid, are oases of bodily comforts in the sunny south in summer. It is quite remarkable how thirsty one can get.

Leading southward from Potenza are a high road and a low road. The latter is narrow and dusty, and for him who goes on foot. It was for me in any case, for it led to my next mountain, Volturino, the highest thereabouts. My attempt upon it will be of particular interest to those who see no point in climbing moun-tains, so I will describe it in some detail.

There are two widely spaced villages on the way. The first,

Abriola, was built on one of those wedge-shaped limestone out-crops that the Apennines go in for. As I approached it looked like the bow of an enormous ship. The houses, trailing back from the sharp bow and spreading to either side above, made the wash. But the ship approached very slowly. I passed below it among woods of stunted oak, the yellowing of the leaves caused more by drought than season. They whispered in the dusty wind and I translated a wish that they might emigrate to England where there would be enough to drink. I sympathized with them.

The second village was Cavello. It was a grim place but it had an inn. When I went on, my one-and-a-half-litre plastic flask was full of red wine. That was enough for the day, surely; but to be on the safe side I determined that I would not drink until I was on the mountain.

Volturino was by this time in full view, and I studied it as I walked to discern the best way up. The eastern ridge—that furthest away from me—was the least steep. So I decided to stick to the road until I had passed beyond the peak, and then strike back. I had an hour or two in which to reach this decision. Then I entered a thick beech forest which covered all the lower slopes and reached halfway up the mountain.

It was delightfully shady under the trees, but I began to regret that I had not picked out landmarks with more care, or better calculated the distance in time. It would be most unfortunate if I turned onto the mountain itself where there were cliffs. I had seen cliffs. But where exactly were they? My field of vision was cut to a hundred yards among the trees. I was not seriously concerned, however, for the road was still going up; and the higher I got by road, the less scrambling or real climbing I would have to do on the mountainside.

Where, turning right-handed, I finally left the road there was an unoccupied charcoal-burner's camp. A charcoal fire had been prepared nearby, but not yet lighted. It was so exact and neat a construction that, except for its size, one would have thought it had been made by insects rather than men. It was beehive-shaped, eight feet high at the apex, and covered with earth except on the windward quadrant. Here, where the wood was exposed (the pieces were too small to be described as logs), one saw the precision with which they had been arranged.

The charcoal-burner's art is still practised extensively in Italy. In any forested landscape one often sees a plume of white smoke to show that these woodmen are at work. The skill has become part of the national heritage. In the half-century of struggle which preceded the Reunification the members of the main secret society were called Carbonari. These men went through a strange and complex initiation ceremony, and very many of them paid with their lives for their resistance to the Spanish and Austrian over-lords. An indulgent modern association is the excellent dish of spaghetti and eggs called carbonara, perhaps because the black pepper with which it is spiced looks something like fragments of charcoal.

Beside the charcoal-burner's fire I sat down to drink my well earned and long-awaited wine. It was sweet.

A good deal shocked, I began to climb the mountain, wondering if Fate had anything even worse in store for me. It had at least a considerable surprise. After scrambling over a little cliff, I found myself on an asphalt road. It was newer than my map, but what it was doing, climbing an uninhabited mountain, I could not imagine. It led eventually to a car park where a family was pic-nicking. Beyond this there was a well made path. It zigzagged up the steep and rocky slope, leaving the woods below it. But at every corner there was a Station of the Cross. Altogether there were fourteen. The last one brought me in sight of the summit. Just below it there was a chapel. Lonely chapels are always marked on Italian maps, and this was an old building, but my cartographer did not appear to have heard of it. Puzzled I climbed on to the summit, and there I stood looking at the tremendous view, then at my map, and then at the view again.

Gradually the realization came. I had climbed the wrong mountain. I had passed below Monte Volturino in the beech woods and turned up the next slope. Volturino was not far off. I could see it clearly. But between me and it there was a great gulf fixed.

I considered the situation for some time, and came to the conclusion that I could not hope for a better view of Volturino, and it was therefore best to leave things as they were.

In the chapel, which was open and unguarded, candles were burning on the altar beside a vase of fresh gladioli. A pile of notes including some of 1,000 lire had been left there. They were an offering to the golden Madonna who reigned over the scene.

When I had descended to Viggiano, more than 3,000 feet below, I was given the explanation. The Madonna spends the winter in the village. On the first Sunday in May she is carried in procession up to the chapel which is called the Santuario del Monte. It must be an exacting pilgrimage, for although there is road or path all the way the climb is steep. I had noticed stone tables at each Station of the Cross. On these the golden Madonna is rested while those who carry her take a breather. The Madonna spends the summer in the mountain sanctuary and on the first Sunday in September is carried down again.

This experience made me thoughtful. In England, where we are still proud of our honesty, the lead on the roofs of village churches is often stolen. But on this lonely summit of the Apennines a gilded statue which must be worth far more than its weight in lead, plus silver plate and a good deal of cash is perfectly safe because the place is sacred.

At the foot of the mountains, near Viggiano and Lago di Pietra del Pertusillo, there were a lot of Roman remains—a bridge with a watchtower, the site of Grumentum, and a good deal of digging going on elsewhere. I went on to Moliterno which was as far as I could get without a rest. It was not a good sleeping place, for there had been a wedding and the young men were driving rapidly round the little town, honking their horns—the modern equivalent of wedding bells. Not until very late did they get tired of this.

The next stage, over the mountains to Lagonegro, about twenty-five miles distant, was the most evocative road walk. An unused road can make one feel more lonely than an untracked mountainside—I suppose because it suggests the presence of human beings, who are not there. To use a conventional phrase in its precise sense, humanity is conspicuous by its absence. But I must start at the beginning.

The road began only a mile or so out of Moliterno. Even there it was a small, modest lane. And a notice said that it was impassable owing to the breaking of a bridge. A man on foot ought to be able to get across any river, but a torrent in a gorge may stop him. An old roadman was digging out a culvert nearby, and I asked him if the way was passable.

'Without difficulties,' he said.

'But that notice —' I began

'I put it there myself. A bridge was swept away by the big storm. Also there was a flood and a landslide.'

'But now the way is passable?'

'I tell you it is without difficulties.'

'So the notice is wrong?'

'It is *not* wrong! I put it there myself. A bridge was swept away by the big storm . . .'

I walked on. At first there were a few cows, then there was

practically no life at all, only some goats and one goatherd dressed in goatskin. Apart from a ruin or two there were no houses. And for whatever reason there were no vehicles until I was almost at the other end, where the road had been repaired. For the rest it was a track with weeds between the ruts. It wound and writhed among craggy mountains—yellow grass, off-white rocks and green spots which were stunted conifers. It was a day of swift clouds and swirling mist. Throughout the middle part of the way, which was high, I was among these troubled vapours. Those lines from the *Ancient Mariner* came into my mind and I repeated them, it seemed endlessly:

> Like one who on a lonesome road
> Doth walk in fear and dread,
> And having once turned round, walks on,
> And turns no more his head
> Because he knows a fearful fiend
> Doth close behind him tread.

I savoured the situation to the full.

In the evening the low sun stabbed under the guard of the clouds like a golden sword. It made the mountains red as blood. But within minutes their colour had bled away, leaving them grey as ashes. I walked down through the twilight to Lagonegro.

I ate and slept in a polished hotel near the Autostrada del Sole. I suppose all the other guests had driven two or three hundred miles that day. But I am sure that I, who had covered not more than twenty-five, had a greater feeling of achievement and of rare experience gained.

Next morning I set out to climb Monte del Papa. I had not seen it yet. It is not visible from Lagonegro which sprouts some midi-skyscrapers and is tucked in under a steep forested slope. But the map showed the Pope's mountain as being well over 6,000 feet and dominating that particular corner of Italy above the Gulf of Policastro. Its summit was likely to provide a view of thirty or forty miles. A long view is worth any amount of trouble to a man who wants to know the country. About forty years ago one could get excellent views from an aeroplane—one of those little open machines which one drove with one's head sticking out above the fuselage. Now, a passenger can scarcely see more from an aircraft than from the loo of a train. Helicopters are no doubt better, but most people have to climb to get a view.

I had to walk several miles before I got an uninterrupted glimpse of the mountain. It had a crouching lion shape, the back or long ridge stretching to my right, to the south. The best way seemed to be up the near hind leg and then along the spine. So I kept to the road until the seventh kilometre stone, then struck up-hill over the railway and under the concrete legs of the half-made autostrada. There was a thousand-foot stretch of bracken and brambles where I had to do a lot of thrashing with my stick. Then I was on the open hillside, scrambling up an outcrop of crystalline rock with slopes of yellow grass to either side.

It was windy, and now and then there would come the tinkle or clonk of bells—sheep or cattle. I could generally see the flock or herd. The puzzle was to spot the man guarding it. At last I would pick him out, crouched in the shelter of a rock. I raised an arm. He raised an arm. There was no other greeting or exchange.

Later on I climbed into a flock of black goats guarded by four white dogs, big and woolly, something like Pyrenean mountain dogs. The Italian shepherd's dog is not meant to regiment the flock, only to guard it from bandits, human and lupine. They set about guarding it from me. But I knew the drill, which is to show a certain purposefulness with one's stick and a readiness to pick up stones. This makes the dogs bark more furiously and therefore be less ready to bite.

Roused by the tumult, the goatherd came from his nook and talked for a few minutes. He had a mild face and a poet's eyes, and he was tolerant when I told him that we do not guard flocks in Britain. He said it would take me another hour to reach the top—which it did.

From the top I would have had an enormous view if the air had not been like watered milk. The sea, which I should have seen clearly, was veiled by it. But looking more steeply downwards everything was clear. I saw little white roads twisting and turning in their efforts to reach a pass. I saw the nascent autostrada using unfair means, tunnels and long-legged viaducts. I saw the curve of hills above the Gulf of Policastro, at the head of which is Sapri.

When, near Eboli, I had paused at the junction of the Rivers Sele and Tanagro I had been within a couple of days' walk of Sapri, which is near to Lagonegro. Instead of going there direct I had wandered for a week on a detour north and east. But thereby I had seen a good deal more of the Apennines, which was the object of the exercise. Once more a conventional phrase is used in its literal sense.

During the final stages of that day's walk one small incident—to be exact, twelve feet high—may be worth mention as demonstrating the typical character of southern Italian mountains. The descent of Monte del Papa was stimulating—first steep slopes of coarse grass and pebbles, then a zone of woodland where one could glissade on rustling dead leaves, then a blessed spring of cold clear water, then five hundred equally steep feet which had been made cultivable by building up a series of stone-walled terraces. The labour involved must have been enormous, but the latest generation of horticulturists had grown tired and allowed the whole to be covered and camouflaged by an entanglement of brambles, what the English call blackberry bushes, the fruit of which many *Meridionali* do not like to eat because the thorns were used to make Christ's crown. Passing through these with high, swift steps I stood on nothing except thorns and fell a dozen feet. I knew what it must feel like for an elephant to fall into an elephant trap.

10

The Sila

My next climb of interest was on Monte Pollino, a massif made up of the Coppola di Paolo and the Serra Dolcedorme. This is a long ridge which averages well over 6,000 feet altitude and dramatically forms part of the border of Basilicata and Lucania.

The first difficulty was to cross the autostrada, here in full operation. They have very efficient fences, as they should. Then it was a case of dodging high-speed cars, then climbing another fence. Beyond there was a stretch of lumpy hills and deep gullies thickly covered with holm oak. The gullies of the limestone Apennines are the very devil. You see what appears to be an unbroken slope in front of you. But having committed yourself to it you find your way cut off by a 300-foot-deep gully gouged out by a miserable little stream. Getting down, across, and up again involves considerable labour.

I reached a larger stream bed, mainly dry at this level, although the flowing water appeared on the surface here and there before going to ground again. The bed was made of powdered white rock and big smooth boulders. But there was greenness to either side, a variety of trees including beech and holly and the white-skinned pine, *Pinus leucodermis*, which is characteristic of Pollino.

Soon the stream was flowing entirely on the surface, lively as a Scottish burn. That is always the most delightful stage when climbing these southern mountains. From the distance they may look desert dry. But water is draining through channels in the

porous rock, and at some stage it bursts out to bound along joy-
ously before it is again absorbed into the hill. The water is cold
and clean, delicious to drink, and vivid greenery crowds about it,
generally hidden at a distance by the shadows of the gorge.

After climbing for a couple of hours I came, above the source
of the stream, to a meadow almost large and flat enough for an
aerodrome. Flocks of sheep were grazing, and the high, strange
cries of shepherds were carried by the wind. Above, there was a
steepish climb through pine trees, then the bare top—small stones
and alpine flowers.

I spoke earlier of a long ridge. Rather it is a hogsback, wide and
smooth. It is very easy to walk on, but how Dolcedorme got its
name I cannot guess, for I would be most surprised if one could
sleep sweetly on it. From up here I should have been able to see
both the Adriatic and Tyrrhenian seas. But it was again a day of
milk-and-water air. What I did see, however, and very clearly, was
how the Apennines almost cease to exist directly to the south of
Pollino. From the Adriatic coast where stood the luxurious ancient
city of Sybiris, an absolutely flat plain stretches inland to cover
more than half the instep of the peninsula, here only sixty miles
across. In the remaining less than half there is a range of mountains,
not high and of necessity narrow, to carry on the Apennines as the
Catena Costiera and to connect with the extensive mass of the
Sila plateau. Between plain and hills is Castrovillari, the only town
of any size for many miles.

To it I descended for the night. In the garden of my hotel was a
cedar tree, one branch extended to my window like a begging
hand. On it lay pretty well everything that can be thrown from a
bedroom window—razor blades, a bunch of bruised grapes, and I
would not like to say what else.

From Castrovillari I went southward by road across the head
of the fertile plain of Sibiri to the foothills of the Sila Greca where

there were three Albanian villages in a row. The Albanian colonies in southern Italy date from the Turkish wars of the fifteenth century. Then a number of ship-loads of Arbereshi (as they call themselves) crossed the Adriatic and set up home, generally in the mountains, in horticulturally poor places where their presence disturbed the local people little or not at all. They built their villages and kept aloof.

They were not always well treated. But nor were the Italians themselves during the centuries of domination by foreign powers. The French oppressed them, the Spaniards oppressed them, the bureaucrats of the Kingdom of Naples got all that they could out of them. But persecution could not break the national spirit of the Albanians.

In the century since Reunification, they have been well and imaginatively treated. But this has not weakened the national spirit any more than the opposite treatment did. They still keep to themselves, speak their own language, observe their own customs.

But there are fewer of them now. At the turn of the century there were said to be eighty Albanian villages in Sicily and the southern part of the peninsula, mainly in Calabria. The total population was estimated at 200,000. Now there are not more than 70,000, in forty villages—still mainly in Calabria. Emigration to America is the main cause of this decline in numbers.

During my brief visit I came across another. The Albanians are said only to marry their compatriots. I talked to a middle-aged woman, intelligent and seemingly quite prosperous. She expressed pride in her race, pride in its language which she said is always talked in the home although the nuns teach in Italian at school. But shortage of work had driven her tailor son to live in Germany, where he had married a German. Intermarriage would soon dilute the communities, although it might be genetically a good thing.

Physically the male Albanians are lean-faced, aquiline; and the women catch the eye chiefly for their traditional dress. They wear the full dress now only for the great *feste,* and I have not seen it. So I quote Peter Gunn's description in his *Southern Italy,* a Collins Companion guide:

> This consists of a long, full skirt, very high-waisted, in the brightest red, green or blue. Both skirt and apron, which from the front appears as the central panel of the skirt, are heavily edged or embroidered in gold. Above this is worn a white blouse of fine linen, and over the shoulders or head a stole, usually of lace. The different coloured dresses glow like a bed of gorgeous tulips.

The first Albanian woman I saw was dressed in black, and leading a donkey laden with green oak branches, presumably to feed her rabbits.

The three villages I visited looked north over the Plain of Sibiri. They were in a row, a few miles apart on the same contour line. (There were no Italian villages within many miles.) They were called San Giorgio Albanese, Viccarizzo Albanese and San Cosino Albanese. The houses were white and often decorated with window boxes. The streets were clean. (This impressed me less when I saw, on leaving, that all the rubbish had been tipped off the road down a steep slope just beyond the last house.) Although there was none of the gaily coloured festal dresses, the old women wore a wide-skirted costume in dark colours. One wondered if the girls will take to this in time or if it will be gone for ever when the old folk die.

All three villages gave a sense of poverty, but not of weary toil. The women gossiped in the market where little except fruit and vegetables were for sale, or at the common pump where they filled their pitchers or plastic containers. The old men sat on their door-steps, the young ones lounged about. One noticed several blind men, and a pathetic old woman walked slowly across the road, pushing a chair in front of her for support. There were plenty of cats and kittens, but few dogs. Apart from the shop- and stall-keepers I saw only three men at work—building a house.

But they must labour in the fields. As the road that led me away went over a pass I looked back down the slope and was struck by the neat appearance of the cultivated land. The soil was as red as Somerset and the precisely planted, carefully weeded olive groves made chess-board patterns of red and green.

South of me now lay the Sila plateau, separated from the coastal range by the valley of the River Crati which flows northward from Cosenza. The anatomy of the Instep of Italy is odd, but not difficult to visualize. The narrow range which rises steeply from the western coast is fairly even in altitude, with the peaks—of between three and four thousand feet—not much disturbing the generally even line of the crest. This is the obvious continuation of the Apennines, the link between the parts of the range north and south. But it is a scrubby thing (in vegetation) and dull, the continuous view of the Tyrrhenean Sea only adding to the monotony created by difficult and unexciting walking. To be frank, I only went onto it twice, had a look and came off it.

This Catena Costiera is only cut off from the Sila by the valley of the Crati as far south as Cosenza. Further south (upstream) the river valley is much less distinct. It soon fades to nothing recognizable as a division, so here the Coastal Range connects uninterruptedly with the Sila—the very much bigger mountain mass to the eastward. In fact the Sila is to the Coastal Range what a gate is to a gatepost.

Thus the Sila must be considered as part of the Apennines. In any case I chose to explore it, or at least to cross it, from end to end, rather than the Coastal Range, because it is much more interesting. Besides, I was already on its fringe at the Albanian villages.

The Sila is a rectangular plateau or tableland approximately thirty miles wide from west to east and forty miles long from north to south. One could go on defining it but it is simpler that the reader should look at a map. But on the map please note two facts. One is that the southern border is a virtual break in the Apennine Chain, in the latitude of Catanzaro where the peninsula is narrowest. The other is that the tableland is remarkably high for such an extensive table of land. The *average* height of this 1,200 square miles area is over 4,000 feet, higher than the highest peak in England or Wales.

As altitude increases, the climate becomes that of a higher latitude. In effect the Sila is a sea-level area a thousand miles north of where it actually is. If a meticulous reader now refers to the earlier statement that the amount of litter depends on latitude, I confirm that there is less litter on the Sila than in the country round about.

A few more general points before embarking on a traverse.

In English spelling, the name is pronounced See-la. This is of some importance. After finishing the walk I wanted to stay at Scilla (the rock that isn't Charybdis on the Strait of Messina) and called at the tourist office in Reggio di Calabria to ask about accommodation. If I had done what I was told I would have gone back to the Sila.

The name derives with little doubt from the Latin *silva,* referring to the woods which in the past were even finer—much more extensive at any rate—than those of the present day. The Romans called the area Silva Bruttia. But there is no evidence that they ever visited the plateau, certainly not in their usual thorough way. When they were busy conquering and absorbing the southern extremity of the peninsula, including the colonies of Magna Graecia, in the third century B.C. onwards, they bypassed the Silva Bruttia, as the Via Appia passed by on the eastern side.

22. Chestnuts and pines of the Calabrian forest.

23. Serra San Bruno.

24. La Cattolica, Stilo.

The Syberites and the Bruttii inhabited the Sila in the earliest days of its history. Then, after the Ancient Roman era, Pope Gregory the Great began using its trees for the woodwork of the numerous churches of Rome. Succeeding Popes continued to do so, but the forests were not massacred until the nineteenth century. Deforestation continued into the present century. Today one sees no tree on the Sila more than fifty years old. Yet there are now many and beautiful trees. There are pines (this is from personal observation) well over 100 feet tall. They are (this is research) *Pinus larico var colabrica*. They smell of resin as a woman may smell of Chanel, but more naturally. On the approach slopes there are olives, oaks, cork trees, poplars. Above, there are large areas of chestnuts and more than all of pines and beech trees. In the swamps—this, instead of the usual calcareous rock of the Apennines, is granite, so there are here and there areas of bog above the impervious rock—in the swamps there are alders, aspens, maples.

I have only seen the flowers in full summer, and on an earlier visit in autumn, so I must go to the books for them. In February the snowdrops appear, scarcely distinguishable in the snow, of which there is much from November until March or April. Then narcissi come into flower, daffodils, violets, pansies and orchids. In June and July the pine woods are strawberry beds. In September and October there are plenty of funghi. Anyone can find them— poisonous and healthy.

Talking of poison, there are vipers. St Patrick never visited the Sila. Mentioning the fauna, I must sadly admit that—as elsewhere on the walk—I met few wild animals, no rare ones at all. So most of the following short list comes from reference books, not per- sonal encounter. There are still wolves. I have met several people who know people who have seen them, though none who has seen them himself. There are wild boars, wild goats, foxes, marmots, **otters**. There are quails, partridges, capercaillie. Perhaps this is not a particularly exciting list, but it shows that the Sila is ample and wild.

On a map—although not very obviously on the ground—the Sila is divided into three parts. In the north is the Sila Greca. This is where most of the Albanian colonies are—hence the name. When the Albanians arrived they were called Greeks, which suggests that the Italians were as lighthearted in their definitions five hundred years ago as they are now. The central, biggest and highest division is the Sila Grande, or Sila Cosentino because it is administered by Cosenza. The southern division is the Sila Piccola, or Catanzarese—of Catanzaro.

From the three Albanian villages in the north, I climbed through high farmland to Acri, a quiet little place with a sanguinary past. In the medieval war between the forces of Anjou and Aragon it resisted the Spaniards until betrayed by a traitor, when it was sacked and burned, and its hero, Nicola Clancioffo, was sawn in half. In 1497 the town was taken by the French, and partly destroyed. In 1799 it suffered during the struggle for existence of the short-lived Parthenopean Republic of Naples. In 1806 it was again almost razed to the ground. This is enough of history to show that the Sila did not always escape invasion, and particularly the trouble that Italy as a whole suffered from for so many centuries, the quarrels of foreign powers for her territory within her territory—like two men fighting over a woman in her drawing room.

From Acri I walked to Lago di Cecita, pretty and girt with trees, and from there to Camigliatello where there are some really splendid pines. But Camigliatello is a budding ski resort with hotels and other buildings going up, which does not at the moment add to its beauty.

I went on over the Botte Donato to the next big lake, Lago

Arvo. This stretch of country provides an excellent example of the topography as a whole. Botte Donato with its 6,000-foot altitude is the highest mountain in the Sila. I will not go so far as to say that you do not notice it, but the walker takes it in his stride, and cars take it in top gear. There is a motor road right over the top and a café-restaurant on the summit where people eat, drink and write picture postcards. The Sila is so high as a whole that its mountains seem scarcely loftier than hills. In this way it is similar to the Campo Imperatore of the Gran Sasso, but in this way only. The Sila is much more clad, more consciously dressed in vegetation. You can easily be alone, with no one in sight; but the work of man is generally visible—in pasture and even plough, in plantation or lumber work. hydro-electric work, houses, all neatly tied up with roads. Nature reigns, but is a figurehead, like a modern monarch.

From Lago Arvo I went to San Giovanni in Fiore. This is surely the most inappropriate name that any town ever had. Admittedly it has some literal justification, for the monastery which was the nucleus of the town was founded by Gioachino da Fiore in 1189. But the only hint of flowers is in the name of this long-dead abbot. The town consists of depressing old houses and ugly new ones. Even the ever-polite T.C.I. guide book cannot bring itself to describe it as *una cittadina graziosa* (the equivalent of saying a woman has a kind heart), commenting only that it is *in bella posizione*.

From Giovanni I made my way southward past the third big lake, Lago Ampollino, and then over the Sila Piccola which is more gashed by gorges than the rest.

The only trouble about walking in the Sila is that the accommodation, although good, is far apart. But the reader has probably noticed a sense of disappointment in this account. I did feel slightly disappointed, although at the time I could not have said why. I had visited the plateau briefly one late autumn fifteen years before, and had a mental picture of blue water and of forests turning golden and bronze with here and there the smoky exclamation mark of a charcoal-burner's fire. On my second visit I saw the lakes again and the forests, only different in that the autumn colours had not yet developed. But I was not fully satisfied.

I summed up in my diary: 'The Sila is the least Italian part of Italy. In the Meridionale it is a quite extraordinary stretch of country to come across. High above the yellow grass of late summer and the rocky, scrubby hills there are great sweeps of verdant green, pine forests, beech forests, chestnuts. The weather is never too hot. One constantly compares the country with the New Forest, the Lake District, Scotland, Norway, Sweden ...' I think that therein lies the explanation. The Sila is not intrinsically Italian, and if it imitates other lands it is bound to do it less well. Why go all the way to southern Italy to see what one can find to perfection in the British Isles or Scandinavia?

Coming down from the south-west corner of the Sila, where it joins the coastal range, and just before reaching what I call—though the maps do not—the Catanzaro gap, I visited Tiriolo. It stands on a steep hillside, overlooking both the Ionian and Tyrrhenian seas. The upper part of its main street has a gradient of one in five. The women have as gay a festal costume as the Albanesi. Even on ordinary days the middle-aged and over are to be seen in the local dress which is full-skirted and has sleeves with many overlapping flaps which give an effect like that of wing feathers. Tiriolo is a very old town. Neolithic, Iron Age and Bronze Age instruments and ornaments have been found in nearby caves, and numerous Roman coins have been picked up. In 1640 a bronze tablet was found. It could be dated as of 186 B.C., and it forbade bacchanalian festivals.

That provides the excuse to end with wine. Unfortunately the wines of Calabria have little to boast of except brute strength. The best is the red Ciro, which comes from the place of that name in the plain beside the Adriatic. Its alcoholic content is about 15 per cent. But one has need of its strength as I discovered before I reached the Toe.

II

Calabria Stern and Wild

As my head came above the ridge the wind struck like a banging door. I dropped on hands and knees and peered between the swaying branches of broom and prickly scrub.

The ground fell steeply to a fertile valley full of olives. So precisely had the trees been planted that they made an exactly chequered pattern of glaucous green on the bare yellow earth. Beyond the grove, the other side of the valley climbed to the ridge on which stands Catanzaro. I had in front of me a suburb studded with huge blocks of flats. A blazing sunset covering half the sky made a fantastic backcloth, and the last rays picked out the functional works of man, making them almost beautiful.

It was delightfully peaceful walking among the olives with no sound of winter wind scolding the evergreen leaves. I came upon a man sitting on a stone, waiting patiently for the end of the world. I greeted him but he did not reply by word or gesture, only stared —a classically featured face under a modern hat. Perhaps the wind was annoyed by this lack of manners, for it whipped off his hat and sent it bowling.

This altered his whole way of life. He was up and running in a moment. No satyr chasing a nymph through a grove ever went faster, and no nymph was ever so elusive. The chase was still on when they passed out of sight.

As I climbed slowly out of the valley I was overtaken by an ox-cart full of children, gay as a litter of fauns. But in the suburbs of

Catanzaro there were endless motor cars and no pavement. I walked a long way in trepidation.

At last I asked an elegant *carabiniere* the way to the Jolly Hotel. He saluted and answered, 'If I told you, Signore, you would not find it. Therefore I will accompany you.' It proved to be at a considerable distance, and he talked all the way with a delight in phrase-making that one associates with the Irish. 'So the Signore does not know Catanzaro,' he said. 'It is a city full of surprises. It is antique and it is new. It is beautiful, ugly, interesting, dull, fascinating and exasperating. It is the finest city in Italy.'

★　　★　　★

That happened in midwinter. When the walk from Top to Toe was no more than an idea at the back of my mind I found myself with a fortnight of holiday in hand over Christmas, and decided to experiment on a section of the range. In my innocence I supposed that the further south I went, the more kindly the weather would be. I finished the experiment with the conviction that in December the four winds blow simultaneously over the Calabrian Apennines, bringing cloud, rain, hail, and snow. But I also came away with the feeling that these wild and handsome mountains deserved to be seen at a better season. Also I had developed a great liking for the Calabresi. They have their faults, which they make no attempt to hide; but they are warm-hearted, friendly and generous to a stranger—as was the *carabiniere* just mentioned. All in all, the idea of the full walk became a firm intention. And when in due time this brought me to Tiriolo, ten miles from Catanzaro, I felt I owed it to the Toe to travel it again. What follows, therefore, is a distillation of the experiences of both winter and summer.

★　　★　　★

Catanzaro and Reggio Calabria, the beginning and end of this double walk, have recently been in the news, squabbling as to which should be the capital of the Region of Calabria. They are each, in any case, the capital of a Province, with Cosenza the capital of the third Calabrian Province.

The last hundred miles of Italy do not—in the larger scale we must now think in—fit with the analogy of a foot. There would have to be only one toe—one spine of mountains—and the coastal outline would suggest corns and carbuncles. So let us forget it. The shape is what it is, and a sketch map conveys it better than words. But it is worth mentioning at the start that this stretch of country is more interesting than much that has gone before. Topographically it is fascinating. The range gradually rises from the Catanzaro gap to the tremendous storm- and earthquake-battered mass of Aspromonte, a fit climax to the long pier of land which by sticking out into the middle of the Mediterranean has so much affected history. Certainly we started above culture and have maintained that level pretty well, but when one gets to the ancient colony of Magna Graecia and a pre-Roman civilization it is impossible to ignore it completely. One other point. This last hundred miles is quite different from the rest of Calabria. The range is here called the Calabrian Apennines as opposed to the Sila and the Catena Costiera. It is a granite range with different topography and variation of vegetation. And the simplest description of the people is that they are more Calabrian than the more northerly inhabitants of the Region.

Before walking on from Catanzaro I made an excursion by transport to visit Maida, an Albanian village a little beyond the middle line of the Catanzaro gap. I had recently read of it in *Ramage in Southern Italy* which is edited by Edith Clay and published by Longmans. Crawford Tait Ramage was a young Scotsman who in 1828 wandered about Calabria on foot and mule-back. It was an adventurous journey, for there were plenty of bandits in those days, but nothing diverted Ramage from his search for 'ancient remains and modern superstitions'.

He thus described the women of Maida: 'Their gowns were richly embroidered, the colours being generally bright blue and purple. Their hair was fantastically arranged, so as to tower above the head like an ancient helmet.' Nothing like that was to be seen by me, but some of the houses were interesting, with complex stucco patterns on the first-floor façade.

Of course Garibaldi had been there. A monument records how in 1860 he and his 3,000 Calabresi captured a listed number of Bourbon guns, rifles and horses. But what should warm a British heart still more is that the vale below Maida was the scene of our first land battle against an army of Napoleon. In 1806 Sir John Stuart made a large-scale commando-type raid, landing with 5,000 men in the Gulf of Eufemia, intercepting General Regnier's army, and defeating it. At this time a new suburb was being built along London's Edgware Road. To commemorate the victory it was named Maida Vale.

A few more words about Ramage, who was my companion on both walks. This first British tourist must have been stared at more than I was. He wrote:

> 'I have a white merino frock-coat, well furnished with capacious pockets, into which I have stuffed my maps and note-books; nankeen trousers, a large-brimmed straw hat, white shoes and an umbrella, a most invaluable article to protect me from the fierceness of the sun's rays.'

The umbrella was then unknown in Calabria: now everybody carries one, particularly the peasants. They use it both in sun and rain. When not in use I have seen a young woman carrying hers on her head—not, unfortunately, on end, but laid flat or at an oblique angle as they carry an empty water jug. A peasant woman automatically puts any burden on her head, even her baby in a basket. Almost invariably their hands are free. Men also have their hands free. They don't carry anything.

Planning my route from Catanzaro, I chose for the first stop a place called Borgia. It looked an easy day's walk and it was marked on my war-time road map with a solid black dot (more important than a ring) which suggested that it should contain an inn. But chiefly I was attracted by its name.

I dropped through the south-western suburbs of Catanzaro by staircase and paved passages, and directly I could do so struck off across country. I was soon forced onto a road. But it was more a pleasant lane than a traffic road and led through olive groves and past fallow fields with open downland behind.

It ended at a T-junction which offered a road either up or down the valley of the River Corace which has its source near Tiriolo. Neither direction was suitable. There was a group of peasants by the road, and I enquired about Borgia. After consultation between themselves they said that it lay beyond the river, which could not be crossed. The rivers of the extreme south have beds which seem absurdly large. There is a barren strip of boulders and shingle as wide as an autostrada, with nothing more than a trickle running down the middle of it. That is how they are for nine-tenths of the year. Then a cloud bursts over the mountains and within an hour boulders and shingle have disappeared under a surging maelstrom of water the colour of the soil. The river is not irrigating, it is sweeping away the topsoil. Standing on its bank, you can also hear rocks rumbling along. If you pass by the mouth of one of these rivers after a storm you will see the sea stained brown or russet or yellow. Of course there are not always storms but also ordinary rainfalls which bring the river up to middle level. That was the state in which I found this one. There were three channels of water in the shingle bed. They were all swift, but it was impossible to judge their depths.

On the bare shingle was a notice saying that it was forbidden to dump rubbish. There was also a lorry with two men who were dumping rubbish. This showed that they were of independent mind, so I asked their advice. They opined that I could get across at a point they indicated. Having said this they got into their lorry and drove away without waiting to see if they were right.

I took off boots and socks, then put on the boots again. The first two streams were easy, hardly wetting my rolled-up trousers. But in the third I was soon waist deep, the current pressing and buffeting, and I had no way of knowing in that turgid water where the depths and comparative shallows lay. Probing with a stick only threw me off balance: in any case I could not safely stand still with the stones moving under my feet. I experienced an uncomfortable minute or two before reaching the further bank.

Hilaire Belloc in *The Road to Rome* tells of a man who St Christophered him across such a river, throwing large stones in front and thus divining the depth. Belloc did not know how this was done, and nor do I, except that presumably a splash in shallow water sounds slightly different from a splash in deep. But there is such a din going on in any case that a remarkably sensitive and experienced ear would be required for this primitive form of echo-sounding.

The men of independent mind had told me that Borgia lay beyond the mountain ahead. They had not said how far beyond, but since they mentioned no intervening place I presumed that it was close. I climbed the mountain and descended to a little road. Following this I came upon a gang of workmen digging out a ditch. They stared at me in a cold, hostile manner reminiscent of Spain, but soon thawed to an even warmer-than-Irish cordiality.

Borgia, which they had at first said was impossibly far away, became closer and closer as they grew more friendly until they told me it was only a few kilometres distant.

Going on more than a few kilometres I saw a village perched on a mountain top, and climbed slowly towards it. The hills were steepening and growing as I went south, with cliffs of sandstone or mud and gullies which seemed incomprehensible unless a giant had gone mad with a spade. I suppose actually it is the result of topsoil erosion leaving the almost treeless earth vulnerable to the gashing water of sudden storms. It was difficult to find useful short cuts.

At the approaches to the village its name was written up— Caraffa di Catanzaro. The ditch diggers had not mentioned this. But what's in a name? I thought. If Caraffa contained a spare bed, a meal and a telephone (I had a long-distance telephone appointment for that evening) it would do. Besides, if there *was* something in a name, this one had a pleasant suggestiveness.

I saw two men standing by a petrol pump, and told them my needs. They were completely negative, so I said *Buona sera* and walked on. I had not gone fifty yards before there was a shout and one of them came running after me. Caraffa contained everything I wanted, he said. No need to go on to Borgia, which was ten kilometres further. He himself would guide me to the hotel.

He took me to a café where we had a glass of wine. Everyone present—all men, of course—were told all about me, for I had been thoroughly cross-examined on the way. We were already the best of friends when I enquired again about the hotel. An awkward silence fell. Gradually, reluctantly, the whole truth came out. There was a hotel. It was pointed out to me. It had a telephone and provided meals. But it was shut. I asked if there was nowhere else. They made the helpless gesture with raised shoulders and spread hands. Caraffa, they apologetically explained, was only a little place. They might have been excusing a child for lack of manners.

I walked on through the night. The rain clouds had cleared away and the sky was splendid with stars. The land was black, but electric constellations of villages glittered from mountain tops. I felt happy and went fast, convinced that everything was going to turn out right. The impression I had gained from my friends in the café was that Borgia was full of hotels.

I had covered rather more than half the distance when a lorry shuddered to a halt beside me and I was invited to get in. The driver was at once passionately interested in my problem and convinced that he could solve it. Borgia was his home town. He would drive me straight to the best hotel.

He stopped outside what looked like a greengrocer's shop. We descended and went in. It was a greengrocer's shop. A pretty young woman dressed completely in black stood at the back of it. She looked very well against all that greenery but she did not answer my questions. The lorry driver on being appealed to said that we were waiting for the *padrona* of the hotel. We waited in silence until an old woman in full mourning arrived and said that everything was *occupato*. There was a good deal of talk, but that was the gist of it.

The driver, still optimistic, invited me to get back into his lorry. He drove me to another 'hotel'. This one was a café. Against a full-blast blaring television which no one looked at (they were too interested in me), but nobody thought of turning down, the explanations and requirements were gone through all over again. This time they took longer because there was one present who spoke English, more or less. So I had first to shout to him and then he shouted a translation. Everyone was extremely friendly. They seemed anxious to keep up the conversation as long as possible. But there was no bed to be had even in a private house, and at the mention of a meal they shook their heads.

I walked on. I had to go right down to the coast to find a place to eat and sleep. Few tourists go inland so there is little accommodation except in the coastal towns.

I climbed back onto the range by Squillace, an ancient fortress on a granite outcrop, the Skylletion of the Greeks and Scolacium of the Romans. This up-and-down progress was hard, but it was interesting because one passed so quickly through different zones of vegetation. Low down there were prickly pears, which the Italians call figs of India. There were groves of oranges and lemons. In the winter fruiting season the groves made wonderfully vivid splashes in the otherwise largely monotone landscape. The orange and lemon are rightly called by their colour alone. There were oleanders, pretty in summer but a dull shrub in winter. The olive trees climbed some way up the hills. Still higher there was bracken and forest, on this first part of the Calabrian Apennines chiefly of stunted oak and sweet chestnut, some of these latter trees with mistletoe growing on them. The general winter colour was russet brown, almost the only green being provided by ilex and cork trees. In summer everything was green high up, wonderfully green although one saw little water. Further along the range there was greenness also in winter, for that is where the fir woods begin, interspersed with beech.

The rivers—from the largest to the smallest—are in their lower courses the barren strips of pebbles and boulders already described. Higher up they are in deep gorges which are extremely laborious to cross. Hardly anywhere, and not for long, is it possible to walk straight across country. The roads and mule tracks are the only practicable ways, and they twist and turn continually. But there is always plenty of interest as one goes along. No one willingly lets you pass without an exchange of news. Now and then you come on a deserted hamlet of half-ruined houses. Were its people killed by a pestilence, driven out by bandits or an earthquake? Imagination, which thrives on walking, has a busy time. Here and there are ruined towers and little fortresses. Norman, Saracen, anti-Saracen? You make up their story, and there is no one to say that you are wrong.

Nearly all the towns and villages are on hilltops—to avoid the *mal aria,* presumably, or for defence. Although both these dangers are of the past, the peasants still live in the populated centre and walk out to work their plots, perhaps many miles away. Commuting was invented long before the word which describes it, long before motors and trains. And the habit dies hard. I was told that where the Cassa per il Mezzogiorno has built suitably spaced farms each surrounded by its piece of land, the peasants don't like it. They miss the doorstep gossip in the evening. They prefer to walk a hundred miles a week.

In the distance the village houses look white, with red roofs. Although few of the buildings appear to be old—in terms of centuries—it is impossible to imagine this rugged land without these red and white oases. They are part of the landscape, built of its stone and earth.

The centre of life is the café for the men, the shop for the women. I never went into a café without becoming involved in conversation. Sometimes it started immediately, as when I ordered a coffee without sugar and the barman asked, 'Are you diabetic?' They are insatiably curious, but with it warm and friendly. And often interesting. Time and again I met people who had been in England, and then it was gratifying to hear that they had been happy (some as prisoners of war). Some had tried their luck in Australia, Canada or the United States. These, of course, spoke English; and then it would have been in the worst possible taste for me to speak Italian. Besides, I was the gainer, for the interpreter being a better conversationalist than I always improved my answers in translation.

Nowhere else in Italy will one meet so many travellers. One bumped into them in the most unlikely places. I went into a village shop and examined the choice of cheese, my staple food. 'Can I help you, sir?' I was asked in perfect English. It was the assistant who had spoken, and before I could answer the *padrone* asked him how he knew that the Signore was English.

'But of course he is,' the assistant answered. 'And yet—perhaps not.' He looked at me with his head on one side as a connoisseur might study a glass of port. 'No, I think he is Scottish, he concluded correctly. This was the more remarkable because Italians call all the inhabitants of the United Kingdom *inglese*.

But this man had been a prisoner of war in Kenya, had served for eleven years in the French Foreign Legion, had been in Australia. I forget where else, but remember he had played for a Scottish football team. He was clearly intelligent as well as experienced, and he was assistant in a little mountain village shop. Calabria is full of talent that it does not use.

So much for a general picture of the country. From Squillace I climbed via Chiaravalle to Serra San Bruno. Serra is the general name of these irregular wooded mountains, and San Bruno was the founder of the Carthusian Order. Although, as far as I am aware, Serra San Bruno is of no administrative importance it is the town—or large village—which impresses one most between Catanzaro and Reggio. It does not date back to the Greeks and Romans—nothing does on the heights. But the Norman King Roger gave the land for the Charterhouse in the year 1090—just twenty-four years after the Norman conquest of England. We have not in this book been much concerned with history, but it is impossible to travel the Meridionale without being impressed by the energy of these northern wanderers, conquerors, administrators. Though few in numbers they left their mark to be seen today in castles, churches and fair-skinned oddities among the populations of Calabria and Sicily.

The present monastery is not easy to visit, impossible for women, for the Carthusians have maintained almost unmodified their strict regime of solitude and prayer. But they have fostered the arts. Serra San Bruno has a superior and independent appearance. In its main street are four churches built of local granite and decorated by local artists. The little town even has an air of gaiety which is scarcely to be found elsewhere. It puts on a show; the fine ironwork balconies possessed by many of the houses, and dating I believe from the seventeenth century, add to the effect, as do the cafés where games of dominoes or cards as noisy as a cup final are always going on.

I ate and slept in the only albergo and was perfectly comfortable. The *padrona* was a big woman, surly and negative at first. Then by some fluke I got through to her, and she told me with shining eyes about her son who was studying medicine in Florence. He had originally intended to go to England. If he had, and if he were at home, he could have talked to me in my own language. She fell silent, contemplating this wonderful possibility.

Incidentally, this *padrona* is one of the very few Calabrian women whom I remember as a personality. On the whole the women know their place, which is in the background; and they do not catch the eye, for they are not beautiful. But somebody must love them, for Calabria keeps its place near the head of the top ten Regions for crimes of passion.

I walked down to Stilo, through foothills torn and scraped by the talons of erosion. Stilo stands on a rock with a background of cliffs. Not until you are close to it do you pick out the tiny Byzantine church. Then the heart jumps with pleasure. It is so surprising, so unlike the thousands of other churches in Italy; and yet it seems just right in that bare ochre landscape. It is is built of warm pink bricks and, in spite of its smallness, has five tile-domed towers, the tallest in the middle, the others at the corners of the square plan. It expresses the pure spirit of early Christian simplicity. Inside, the custodian tells you that it is full of symbolism with its four pillars of different stone. But simple sincerity is the abiding impression given by this delightful church, called Cattolica to express universality.

I would have liked to walk across the face of the slope to Gerace, the next place I really wanted to see. It was at the same altitude and as far inland as Stilo. But it is not practical to follow a contour in that contorted land. One must either descend to the coast where there is a railway and a big road and everything looks alike, or one must climb to somewhere near the ridge. That is what I did.

On the way I visited Ferdinandea. It was built as a summer palace—a grand name for the farm-like building—by Ferdinand II of Naples. It also had an iron foundry which they say produced the first Calabrian cannon. But later Garibaldi slept there and it is now associated with his name. For me its charm was its silence and its thick forest. From its lake there ran a little stream in which I cooled my wine.

Following the high roads—high in altitude, I mean—had developed a peculiar charm which has remained in memory. I think it was the beech trees which began it. Still, when half asleep in bed, I sometimes follow those strange roads with a steep slope on one side and a steep drop on the other, wandering solitary and apparently purposeless, the silence broken only by the blow of an axe on wood or the shrill klaxon cry of a modern charioteer driving his 500 c.c. horses at reckless speed with screaming tyres.

My way led towards the steep valley of the River Torbido. Approaching Grotteria the road zigzagged down an actual cliff.

If you fell off a zig you would land on the zag below. But I was overtaken by an articulated tanker weighing Supercortemaggiore knows how many tons.

Grotteria clings to the same cliff lower down. Because of the steepness of the slope you can from above see the whole town at once, as you can see a whole theatre from the gods. 'What do the people live on?' I asked the barman when I stopped for a drink. 'La terra,' he answered briefly. There was more rock than soil.

On a terrace below a woman was in hysterics, screaming a flood of indistinguishable words, swaying her body forward and back, her arms outflung, her long and tousled hair swinging and swirling like seaweed as the tide comes in. A crowd had gathered to stare. They stood silent and unexpressive as people watching a house being built. They held up the traffic. I asked the driver of a Roma car what the trouble was. 'Her husband has died,' he answered bitterly. 'These creatures martyr themselves.'

Gerace is near the beginning of the next trans-peninsula road. This goes over the Apennines by what is called the Passo dei Mercanti. Gerace is another little city built upon a rock. From below, its fortress-like appearance is most striking. It must have been a hard place to capture, but it could not resist earthquakes. No building older than the Norman period has survived. But earthquakes could not destroy the Greek language which was spoken there, I have read, until 1480. The cathedral is said to be the largest in Calabria—excepting, one must suppose, the big, new, clinically clean and unsympathetic Cathedral of Catanzaro, which replaces the one we bombed out in the war. Gerace's cathedral is Norman, Romanesque—whatever you like, for earthquakes and reconstruction have considerably modified it. Still, it remains a splendid and dignified building.

There are several other ancient churches in this strange little town. The streets are narrow and cobbled, the side streets sometimes only a few yards in extent. But most of them have long names. Gerace with its entrance under an arch and its shut-away *piazza* evokes a strong feeling of the troubled past. One can see the merchants taking refreshment there, arranging for an escort before crossing the high and lonely pass on the way to the plain of Gioia Tauro. It was thus throughout history. Ramage experienced the echoes of it. He went, 'mounted on one of the sure-footed ponies of the country'. He wrote, 'The Passo dei Mercanti . . . is beset with robbers.' Much against his will he was prevailed upon to take a guard of four armed men. It had been his intention to depend only on his umbrella as a defence against brigands. 'As they are probably unacquainted with such an article, they might imagine it some deadly weapon of war, and take fright.'

The road twisted and turned as it climbed to the Merchants' Pass. Sometimes it balanced precariously on the edge of an abyss. I took a short cut across a steep valley—short in distance but great in the effort demanded. At the bottom I came upon what had been a car until it went over the edge. Poor thing, it was scarcely recognizable as a once mechanical thing.

When I regained the road a sleet storm hit me in the face. I felt lonely, tired, very uncomfortable; and I realized that it was still a long, long way to Cittanova—the first place which might offer shelter.

I was thus in the depth of gloom when I was accosted by two modern Calabrian bandits. They were in a little van. The driver was tough and middle-aged, his passenger a cunning-looking old rascal—what the Italians call *un furbo*. I told the driver that he was very courteous to stop for me; and he replied that when one had a chance to do a favour one was glad of the opportunity.

After this scrupulously polite beginning the *furbo* started putting me through the questionnaire. When he came to why I was doing what I was I replied with a laugh that all *inglesi* are a little mad. I suppose the driver thought I had been embarrassed. At any rate he exploded in the face of the *furbo*. In a passion he demanded what right he had to ask questions like that. He swung round and pointed his right hand at me, meanwhile steering from memory with his left. 'This Signore is a foreigner,' he shouted. 'He is a courteous Signore and he is our guest. He deserves to be treated courteously. But you—you—man, you question him like a murder suspect.' He shook his fist in the *furbo*'s face, then raised his arms on high. 'Santa Madonna! We are Christians, aren't we? It is the duty of Christians to help each other. But you—you—man . . .'

All this was at increased speed, for in his fury the driver stamped on the accelerator. The *furbo* only grinned, which made the driver angrier than ever. I sat, fascinated and helpless, on some old tyres at the back.

When I left them they both got out of the van, shook hands and wished me 'Buon viaggio'. The quarrel had blown over as quickly as it had arisen. It was similar to those frequent incidents in a café game of cards when murder seems on the point of being done, but which are only a post-mortem of the last hand.

The meteorological storm did not end so quickly. I walked through wet snow with my trousers sticking to my legs, still half a dozen miles from Cittanova.

Cittanova appeared through the snowflakes as an expanse of dim electric bulbs. It was a sprawling overgrown village and I could not find its centre. The inhabitants were not in the streets in that weather. But I saw a peasant woman, caught up with her and addressed her politely, 'Scusi, Signora—' She screamed and ran away. Later I found a man who put me on a long, straight street at the end of which, he said, I would find an albergo.

The place had 'Hotel' written over the door, but the windows were dark. As I went in there was a shout of 'Chi è?' I shouted back, 'Sono io'—I am I. 'Ma chi è?' Guided by these questions I found the kitchen where an old man and two women sat close round a small table under which there was a charcoal brazier, it and their lower halves curtained by the drooping cloth. I was invited to join them. It was a quarter of an hour before one of the women plucked up courage to take her legs out of the warmth and guide me up a stone staircase to a room which was furnished with a bed, a basin and a notice stating that it was forbidden to spit on the floor.

Nothing was said about a meal. So I brewed up coffee with my baby immersion heater, which plugs in like a razor, and drank it with a dash of brandy. Thus centrally heated, I dined on bread, cheese and wine from my haversack—to the accompaniment of a violent thunderstorm. Shouts of 'Che fulmine!' rang through the house and all the lights of Cittanova went out.

12

Aspromonte

The Passo dei Mercanti is the last pass in the range before you come under the influence of Aspromonte. It is a great mass of a mountain with broad shoulders but no apparent head. The name, so the wise men say, comes from the Greek *aspros,* white. One feels that that is being a little bit too clever. Certainly the mountain is white in winter, but that is no distinction in the Apennines. And after all it is in Italy, not Greece. Why should it not derive from the Italian *aspro,* which means harsh, rude, rough?—presumably because that would be too simple. Etymologists have reputations to keep up.

In any case the name covers the whole mountain mass. The actual summit, a forested lump scarcely to be distinguished from a number of others, is called Montalto (derived, presumably, from *monte,* a Spanish card game, and the English word meaning counter-tenor or contralto). Its altitude is 6,420 feet. It is not a mountaineer's mountain, for although its summit is difficult to locate you can climb it with your hands in your pockets. But my 1908 Baedeker takes it seriously, saying that the tourist should allow a day and a half for the excursion, starting early on a moonlight night with a guide and two mules.

To me it is a lovable mountain. It gives the impression of having had a bad time during the last few million years. It stands there on its thirty-mile-diameter base, looking across the Strait of Messina at Etna, wishing that it also was a volcano with beautiful curves instead of being a chronic sufferer from earthquakes which have left it a geological wreck. Yet it puts a brave face on it and manages to be beautiful in parts, very wild in parts, and tame in none—except possibly its ski resort. It is full of surprises:

> Age cannot weary her, nor custom stale
> Her infinite variety.

What more can one ask of a mountain, or Egypt's queen?

Then there is Aspromonte's association with the human race. Appropriately, the greatest Italian walker of all time visited it twice, once after his conquest of Sicily with the Thousand in 1860, and—less gloriously but most interestingly—two years later. But the profession Aspromonte is really famous for is banditry. Before 1850 the annual number of homicides in the course of robbery or of eliminating police informers must have exceeded a hundred, perhaps hundreds. Precise figures were not kept while the Bourbons ruled in Naples. Banditry continued to flourish in the early decades of this century. Benedetto Musolino (not to be confused with Benito Mussolini), who was born and worked on Aspromonte, shot to death fifteen informers, certain, plus three possible who crawled away. 'Ah, if you could have seen him, sir,' a *contadino* said to Norman Douglas. 'He was young, with curly fair hair (a descendant of the Normans), and a face like a rose. God alone knows how many poor people he helped in their distress. And any young girl he met in the mountains he would help with her load and accompany as far as her home, right into her father's house, which none of us would have risked, however much we might have liked it. But everyone knew that he was pure as an angel.'

Benedetto Musolino is still remembered as a Robin Hood on Aspromonte. He died in a prison asylum not many years ago. One of his incidental benefactions to the area was the establishment of telegraphic communications: they were set up in the attempt to catch him. It is remarkable how recently the bandit not only flourished but was accepted—if not approved—on the mountain. In *Old Calabria,* published in 1915, from which the above is quoted, Norman Douglas tells of how he declined the offer of a charming local youth to guide him across Aspromonte even though the young man was prepared to hand over his knife. A second knife might be tucked away, and bodies could be so easily concealed in those forests, gorges and scrub thickets that it was a spare-time occupation to kill strangers on the off chance of finding a few pennies in their pockets. Douglas was no chicken heart, and he was a formidable walker. He says that a crossing of Aspromonte is by no means to be recommended to young boys or persons of delicate health. He calls the mountain the Storm Gatherer and does not associate himself with a Greek derivation of the name, though he conversed in Byzantine Greek with some of the mountain villagers.

Finally among these generalities, Aspromonte is far and away the best area for *fiumare,* the broad torrent beds already referred to. In spring thaws they carry off the winter snows at full gallop: in summer they carry off the storm water, and the soil. Look at a map of Aspromonte. It is patterned by radial blue lines. To convey what they really stand for they should be lines of foaming brown. The Cassa per il Mezzogiorno cannot do anything about it. Nobody can, with the possible exception of God. The *contadini* of Aspromonte live much the same hard lives that they always have. The wonder is that they have given up banditry. Aspromonte remains in character a bandit mountain made for poets—although no poet has written of it.

I approached it from the north in winter, from the south in summer. On both occasions I wandered about a good deal. I will attempt a description of personal experiences on it.

From Cittanova I descended by the merchants' road to the Plain of Gioia Tauro. This was less for the sake of giving Aspromonte a fair chance by approaching it from sea level than because I wanted to see La Piana which is one of the most fertile plains in southern Italy. In Taurianova I was caught by a violent thunderstorm, and took shelter in a barber's shop, explaining that I did not want my hair cut but only to get out of the rain. 'S'accomodi,' said the barber with a bow and a sweep of the arm. And then he asked, 'Will you have a coffee, a beer or an aperitif?'

'Surely you do not sell such things,' I said.

'Naturally I do not *sell* them,' he answered. 'I am offering you refreshment.'

Directly the storm was over, the apprentice who swept up the hair was sent running to the nearest café. I remembered Ramage's remark about the *Meridionali* a hundred and forty years ago. 'Whatever may be the vices of the Italians, I think you will allow that they are not deficient in hospitality and kindness to strangers.'

A few hours later I was thinking about his journey again, for like him I passed through the olive groves of La Piana. The trees were as big as half-grown oaks. They were magnificent, with straight, clean bowls and symmetrical branches. There was none of the usual dilapidated picturesqueness. Ramage made a similar observation, and I wondered if I might be looking at some of the actual trees he saw, for the olive, symbol of peace, wisdom, abundance and glory, may live a thousand years. One thing is certain, modern agriculture cannot claim credit for this outstanding growth. Here and there a towering umbrella pine, a giant even among these olives, spread out its arms of darker green in benediction. And the ground beneath the trees was carpeted with delicate ferns.

In such scenes of vegetable splendour it was saddening that the only human beings about were peasant women in their thick rough skirts and shaggy shawls, picking up windfall olive fruits at the roadside. Bent completely double and shuffling along, their back views looked like those of grazing goats.

I was muttering something pessimistic about the dignity of man when I was startled by a loud and cheerful horn. I turned to see a break-down truck drawing up beside me. Out of the cab window leaned a smiling young god Pan with curly black hair and blue eyes.

'You are English,' he said. (It was a statement, not a question.) 'I knew it from your back side. Please get in.'

I got in with my telltale walking stick, haversack and pipe.

'Where did you learn the language?' I asked.

'In Australia. I came back last month.'

'What were you doing in Australia?'

'I was a mechanic,' he said.

'And here?'

'I am a mechanic.' He smiled in a way that would have knocked any nice girl off her moral balance. He was certainly the descendant of a faun and a shepherdess. He was about twenty-three years old, and had gone to Australia and come back again as one might visit the local town.

'Will you enjoy being a mechanic here?' I asked.

'I was born here,' he said, in complete explanation.

He asked me what I did for a living. I never admit to writing if I can help it. When one does, people tend either to shut up or put on an act. So I said I worked in an office.

'I knew it!' he exclaimed excitedly. 'I was sure of it as soon as I saw your face.'

Shocked, I asked why he had been sure.

'I could see you were intelligent,' he said.

This man whose skilful hands had taken him half round the

world was modest at the thought of an office desk. One man's idea of dignity, I thought. Poor young god Pan!

I reached Delianova. One wondered why so many of these old-looking places called themselves new. This one showed an attachment to the past, or at least a respect for it. On a wall was a portrait of Mussolini in aggressive, confident half-profile. Mussolini did not do very much for the *Meridionali,* less than he did for Rome and the North—draining the Pontine Marshes, for instance. But he did something for them in his early days of power, and it is surely to their credit that they do not deface the picture of a lost leader because he finally let them down. They are no more Fascist than is the rest of Italy, but I do not believe that Calabria would have hung up a man and his mistress by the heels as did the enlightened North. I am not concerned with politics, only good manners.

In my *albergo* that evening the only other guests were a young couple from Turin, and we got into conversation. I told them how well I had been treated in Calabria. The young man then told me that I had been deceived. The *Meridionali* were false, lazy, dishonest, squandering all the money that was spent on them by the North. The waiter, a *Meridionale* from his jet-black hair to his tiny feet, stood by the table looking hurt but saying nothing. I launched into a hot defence of the Calabrians. The waiter looked at me with shy gratitude, but still said nothing. Rich relatives and poor relatives do not love each other more for charity given and received.

Climbing Aspromonte one is struck by the woods and by the terraces. The woods, which really deserve to be called forests, are of beeches, oaks and other deciduous trees, and in a few places of magnificent pines. But the terraces are the more distinctive feature. You climb very steeply for a thousand feet or so, and then you are on a great flat plain. This is not necessarily covered by trees. There are heaths and scrub areas and some rough agricultural land. Such buildings as there are tell you of the poverty of the people who gain their living from this land. But the visual impression is that you are on a plain—until you come to the next steep slope. Each terrace, which may be scores of square miles in extent, has its subtly different climate and vegetation, and different views. This is part of the infinite variety. It is a long country spread upwards instead of laterally.

Climbing from Delianuova there are at first thick woods of not particularly distinguished trees, then prairie-plateau; and then, a few miles before Gambarie, pine forest. The best views are southward—behind one—over the plain of Gioia Tauro. In no other direction can one see any distance. And of course the plain disappears soon after reaching the first terrace lip. It is strange country, not beautiful but in wild weather awe-inspiring. It would be quite easy for a man alone to be killed here in winter, not by bandits but exposure. And nobody would find his body.

The pine woods are grand and dignified. Among them, a few miles from Gambaria, is a Garibaldi museum which the guide book tells you not to miss. It was shut on both occasions that I visited it. Winter should be quite as much the season as summer, for Gambaria is a ski resort, with several hotels and a number of villas, chiefly used by the people of Reggio at weekends.

Deep in the pine woods, not far from the museum, is a *cippo* or small monument recording the fact that Garibaldi was wounded here in 1862. It was a strange, unhappy affair, for the national hero was wounded by his compatriots.

King Victor Emmanuel, who owed the throne of Italy to Garibaldi more than to any other single person, was none the less embarrassed by the impetuous and undiplomatic single-mindedness of his general. After Garibaldi's meteoric conquest of Sicily and Naples in 1860, the king marched south, less to join forces with him than to prevent him from liberating Rome from the temporal rule of the Pope and his cardinals—which would have upset the Catholic powers. So the Papal States remained outside reunited Italy, and Garibaldi returned to his farm on Caprera. But two years later he was back in Sicily, raising an army of enthusiastic volunteers with the battle cry 'Rome or Death'. The king sent a force to stop him, and on this occasion unfortunately did not lead it himself.

The two forces met on Aspromonte on an afternoon in July. It was a difficult situation for the intensely loyal liberator. I have come across a letter he wrote a few days later:

> I ran along the front of our line crying out to them not to fire, and from the centre to the left, where my voice and those of my aides-de-camp could be heard, not a trigger was pulled. It was not thus on the attacking side. Having arrived at a distance of 200 metres, they began a tremendous fire, and the party of Bersaglieri who were in front of me, directing their shots against me, struck me with two balls, one in the left thigh, not serious, the other in the ankle of the right foot, making a serious wound.
>
> All this happened at the opening of the conflict, and I was carried to the skirt of the wood after being wounded, I could see nothing more, a dense crowd having formed round me while my wound was being dressed . . . As there was no firing on our side it was easy for the troops to approach and mingle with ours, and when I was told that they wished to disarm us I replied that they should themselves be disarmed.

One is left (from another source) with the picture of Garibaldi sitting with his back against a pine tree, smoking a cigar, while the officers of both sides stand around arguing as to what should be done next.

Before leaving the battlefield I must tell of an interesting scene which I saw there myself in summer. Jeep-loads of armed *carabinieri* were all over the place. What was evidently a field headquarters had been set up with wireless aerial and all, and a helicopter was literally hanging about. I, apparently the only person unarmed and not in uniform within miles, was consumed with curiosity but dared not ask these preoccupied police what it was all about.

An Italian friend who had read about it in the newspapers told me afterwards. The *carabinieri* had received word that the Mafia, Sicilian and local, were holding some sort of reunion-cum-conference, appropriately on Aspromonte. There was a chance of rounding up the whole lot. In fact nobody was rounded up on the perfect bandit mountain. But I can't help wishing I had been arrested. One could have dined out on the story for years. I felt let down, for I *was* arrested in the Pyrenees.

★   ★   ★

I did not climb Montalto in winter. It could have been done, but it would have involved a weary knee-deep slog through snow So I reserved the climax for a summer climate. Then I approached Aspromonte from the south, having covered the preliminary thirty or forty miles by transport.

There is a railway and a whacking great road all round the coast of the peninsula. Between Catanzaro Lido and Capo Spartivento it is called the Costa Jonica or Ionica because the coast faces the Ionian Sea and Italians do not differentiate between an I and a J. From Spartivento to Capo dell'Armi (both splendid names), where the coast turns north for the Strait of Messina, it is now called the Jasmine Riviera. This is one of those tourist gimmicks which every Mediterranean land has been practising with more or less imagination for the last thirty years. Having run out of colours for coasts they have to make do with smells. Anyway, they all look the same—a string of bathing resorts. You like them or you don't. A book about mountains should not judge. But at Melito, near the Capo dell'Armi, you may turn north along a little mountain road which is quite fascinating.

The first place you come to is Pentedattilo. One can't get away from the Greek derivation here, although one questions the guide-book statement that the rock looks like the five fingers of a hand. It would be a sadly deformed hand, and the rock is not real rock at all. It is the roughest sort of conglomerate. If any gymnast climber is tempted to attempt it, good luck to him! The stones would come away in his hand and the whole thing is well spiced with cactuses.

The real interest is in the two villages. The old, picturesque insanitary one is just below the hand. In it I met only a dilapidated old woman who started talking but soon lapsed into an unintelligible whine, a pig, a dog, a rabbit and a quantity of lizards who alone of the population were made lively by the sun. The old village is dying. You can see, feel, smell it as you climb its steep stony and dusty streets. The church is in sad disrepair. Above its door three words of a notice remain, 'Bestemmie e Turpiloquio'. Presumably the word meaning forbidden has been rubbed out. It struck me as a notice which only suggests what was not intended, for one does not naturally visit a church to blaspheme and use bad language.

The new village is a cluster of concrete boxes half a mile away. 'But it is not complete yet,' said the roadman. 'It has no church.' Then he started talking of his endless and unrewarding job. 'You do not have rough roads like this in England,' he said. 'I once saw a picture of an English road.'

While I ate lunch and talked with him an old couple came by, going from the new village to the old. The woman was carrying a fragrant bunch of herbs, and gave me a sprig. I asked what it was. 'Basilico,' she said. I told her I had not recognized it because it was so much bigger and better than the basil which grew in my garden. This pleased her so much that she gave me the whole lot. I was left sitting in the sun beside the roadman, much moved and wondering what to do with a large bunch of wilting herbs.

I carried it up Aspromonte, and it turned to compost in my rucksack. The southern ascent is finer than the northern. There were occasional splendid views of the Strait of Messina with an endless procession of ships puffing along in both directions, their sailors apparently undistracted by Scilla and Charybdis. There were similar terrace plains, seemingly more fertile than those of the northern side, but this may well have been a matter of season. There were splendid beech woods, here and there with a monarch tree blown over, roots in the air, to remind one of the storms of winter. And there was a spring of perfectly delicious water gushing in careless generosity from the bosom of the mountain.

I slept at Gambarie. Montalto is about seven miles from there, but at the end of a long project extravagance is appropriate. I got up earlier than I care to mention and began to climb. It was nearly all by forest road, which was just as well for it was dark. Trees are strange companions in the dark—strange but sympathetic, for you can make whatever characters you like of them. A mile or two before the summit I passed an American radar station, but did not stop to ask for top security coffee. Anyway, they all appeared to be asleep. There is a strange joy in being the only person awake in a sleeping world.

I left the road and pushed through wind-blown beech trees to the top. It is an impressive summit, particularly in the dark. I was lucky to hit it off. The only sign that I was likely to be right was that there was the ruined foundation of a monument. I had read that a golden statue of the Redeemer stood lifting arms of bene-diction over Reggio. Certainly there was no statue, but it was unlikely there would be two foundations.

I learned later that the statue had for the second time been blown down by a storm, and removed (goodness knows how!) for repair. This information finally convinced me of what I have long suspected. God no longer has anything to do with the weather. He has left it to some angelic bureaucrat who arranges it according to a stereotyped and totally unimaginative pattern.

I walked up and down, shivering and waiting for the dawn. Everyone has waited for a dawn, actual or metaphorical, and how long they both take! There are so many signs and hopes before anything actually happens. But at long last there came the moment of clarity with the sun bubbling up over the forested heights behind me, Sicily and the little islands of Lipari growing momently more crystal clear in front.

I sat down on a stone and lit my pipe. I looked over the falling land, over the Strait of Messina, over part of Sicily and over the still almost colourless water to the north.

I counted three volcanoes. There was Etna, of course. To the right was the island called Vulcano which discreetly belched vapour, and still further to the right the unmistakable exclamation mark of Stromboli.

We sat there smoking together, those three volcanoes and I, for perhaps ten minutes. Then I got up and started the long walk down to Reggio di Calabria, the Toe of the Peninsula.

INDEX

INDEX